Musicarta

KEY CHORDS

Volume One

THE FIRST FOUR CHORDS

(I, IV, V and vi)

R A Chappell

Foreword

This Musicarta Key Chords workbook tackles three simple but vital questions: What chords go together best? Which chords should I learn first? What's the best way to learn them? The workbook explains the musical key and then presents a way of building chord vocabulary by learning the first four 'key chords' in a methodical way.

(Key chords are the simple chords that can be made from the unaltered notes of a scale. In academic music theory, they are known as diatonic chords.)

Each Key Chords module adds another chord change to your repertoire, demonstrated and rehearsed in popular keyboard style riffs and studies and with numerous illustrations and full audio and MIDI support (optional free download).

The syncopation skills that turn simple chord sequences into pop/rock music and improvisation are taught in progressive 'build-ups' which ensure you always come away from a session with a sense of accomplishment and a riff of some description at your fingertips.

The Key Chords programme will also develop your musical ear. A large percentage of popular music is built out of the four chords covered in this volume – not only will you learn to play them, but you will with practice find yourself being able to tell just by listening what chords are being used in lots of mainstream popular music.

Free support material download

Send your proof of purchase (Amazon transaction ID) to webmaster@musicarta.com and you will receive a coupon for your free support material download. The download comprises:

- The Key Chords module audio and MIDI files
- The 'MidiPiano' virtual keyboard MIDI file player (Windows OS), and
- A folder containing other helpful resources.

In order to get the most out of your Key Chords purchase, follow the steps in the next section of this book, 'Preparing to Learn'.

About Musicarta

The Key Chords Vol. 1 workbook was originally the 'Chord Progressions' series of web pages at www.musicarta.com, a website dedicated to developing musical creativity and popular music keyboard skills. You can find additional interactive chords-focussed learning material on the site via the Chords navbar tab, and also on the 'Mister Musicarta' site YouTube channel.

The chord sequences in this volume are, in the author's view, generic, and any resemblance to others' work is the result of their demonstrable ubiquity. This material in this volume is copyright the author, R A Chappell. Please respect copyright and do not duplicate this material except for 'fair use' study purposes.

Table of contents

MUSICARTA KEY CHORDS

Preparing to Learn

This module is about organising your resources for efficient learning, and assumes you have downloaded the Key Chords digital learning support material. (Email your Amazon purchase transaction ID to webmaster@musicarta.com for your free download coupon.)

Now organise your resources for efficient learning. A little time spent in advance will pay off in multiples over your course of study. Tick the checklist boxes as you prepare to start studying the modules.

☐ On your computer, make a master Key Chords folder

Audio and MIDI support files

Nearly every musical example in the Key Chords comes with audio and MIDI support, so you can hear-and-see what to play without having to read music.

Each example has a table below it:

KCA_1_01	KCM_1_01

Audio files for musical examples are named in the left hand table cell under the examples. They are always labelled KCA, for Key Chords Audio, then a module number (1, 2) and a running order number, e.g. KCA_1_01. MIDI files are numbered the same way but start KCM for Key Chords MIDI.

Note that examples do not always have both audio and MIDI files.

Your audio and MIDI files are grouped in folders by module in a zipped folder called Key Chords audio + MIDI.

☐ Put the Key Chords audio + MIDI folders in your master Key Chords folder. (Leave them in the folders they come in.)

Your audio files are MP3-encoded. Practically all media players will play them. Leave your audio and MIDI files in the module/supplement folders they came in.

MIDI files are computer-code music files. They can be played in many computer music applications. (Your computer media player will probably be able to play them as base-standard audio files.)

To take full advantage of these MIDI files, Musicarta strongly recommends that you install and learn to use the free MidiPiano 'virtual piano' included in the download. MidiPiano is simple to use, and shows the music in the MIDI file being performed on a virtual piano keyboard and scrolling past in a 'piano roll' pane as it plays.

This is a great help in learning and practicing. Musicarta strongly recommends you take the time to install and learn to use MidiPiano. Full instructions and alternative MidiPiano download locations can be found on the Musicarta 'MidiPiano' web page (navbar tab).

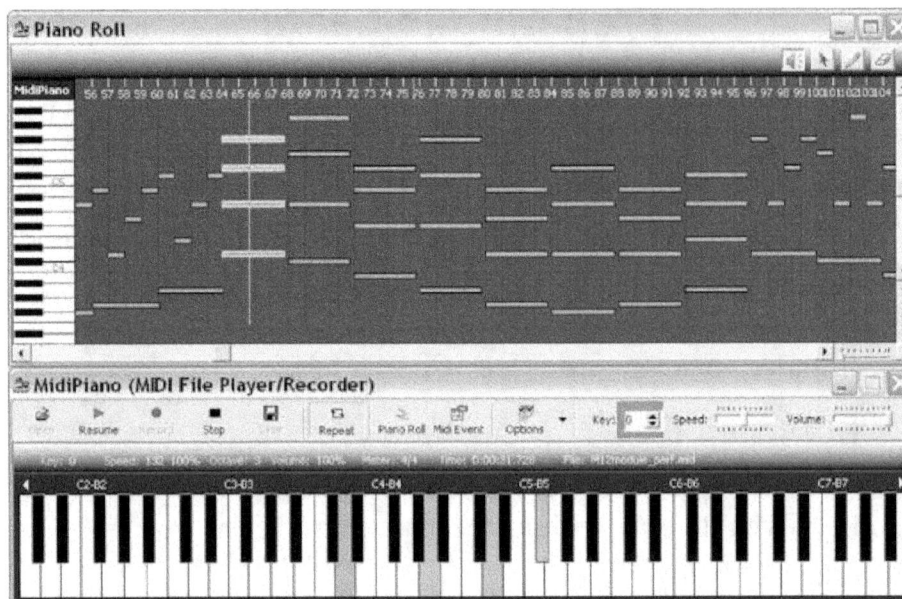

MidiPiano is a Windows XP/Windows 7 application only. There are free virtual pianos for all platforms available on the Internet – Synthesia is a good Mac-compatible alternative. You can use sequencing software like Sonar or Cubase to view and listen to MIDI files, but MidiPiano's piano roll display is by far the best option.

□ Install and learn to operate MidiPiano or Synthesia.

Other audio resources

While you are working through the Key Chords workbook, get into the habit of playing along with audio.

□ Arrange you playback devices so you can operate them from your piano stool.

YouTube hosts numerous pop standard videos and these are excellent free reference material.

□ Organise favourite YouTube video bookmarks in your internet browser.

(Musicarta makes no assertions concerning the legality of any YouTube material.)

Early pop music is a rich source of songs relying heavily on the four chords covered in this first volume of Musicarta Key Chords. Make a point of listening to radio 'golden oldies' programmes, and dust off your old '60's Classics' etc. compilation CDs.

□ Timetable radio shows and source 'golden oldies' reference material.

Recognising by ear what chords are being played in music is very satisfying, and your ability able to 'just sit down and play' will improve in parallel. (Note that you don't have to be at the keyboard for this 'focussed listening'.)

Backing tracks and Audacity

As well as being a lot of fun, playing along with a recording, a chord backing track or a drum/rhythm section track is a great stimulus to 'keeping the notes coming'.

You can use any Key Chords audio as a backing track. Musicarta Key Chords Vol.1 also provides a selection of drum tracks to support your practice and inspire your improvisations. Music examples which have a particular recommended drum track have a three-cell table underneath:

KCA_1_01	KCM_1_01	(drum track ref. here)

Musicarta recommends 'Audacity' (R), a simple, reliable and free sound editor which can 'loop' (repeat) audio tracks seamlessly, for playing backing tracks while you practice and improvise.

To loop in Audacity, all you have to do is launch the application, 'open' your backing track sound file in the normal way, and press shift+spacebar.

☐ Download and install Audacity and practice 'looping' a backing track.

Windows Media Player will also repeat audio tracks, but not as accurately. The keyboard shortcut is Control + T; the menu command is in the Play drop-down menu and there is an arrowed circle repeat button on the control bar at the bottom of the player window.

☐ Find the 'repeat' controls on your media player.

Some media players can also slow down a performance without changing the pitch. This is a great practice boon – make sure you know how to do it.

☐ Learn how to slow down a performance on your media player.

MidiPiano can also slow down MIDI file performances. See above for details.

Know your desktop

When you are studying with Musicarta Key Chords you will typically need three windows open:

- The audio and MIDI folders for the module you're studying;
- MidiPiano; and
- Your computer media player.

Get into the habit of opening these quickly and arranging them on your desktop so you can find them and cycle between them easily. Learn relevant keyboard shortcuts.

Practice issues

Musicians are often deterred from practicing by practice privacy issues. An electronic keyboard with headphones can solve this problem. Moving a real piano out of the family TV lounge is another obvious improvement!

If you have a real piano, you can listen to Key Chords audio tracks with earphones or headphones and still hear yourself play at the same time. If you have an electronic keyboard, you can listen to your backing track on earphones and listen to your keyboard on headphones over those, and play along to a backing track in complete privacy.

☐ Address practise privacy issues.

Other Musicarta resources online

Musicarta's 'MisterMusicarta' YouTube channel hosts videos showcasing Key Chords material. There are also many resources at the main www.musicarta.com site to support your learning and encourage keyboard creativity in all its aspects.

☐ Bookmark www.musicarta.com and the MisterMusicarta video channel.

Know your chords (and keys)

The three-note right hand chords we will mostly be working with in this series of lessons come in three 'flavors' – root position, first inversion and second inversion. They are made of the same three notes but 'flipped' to put a different note at the top.

Musicarta uses a circle/square/triangle symbol shorthand to indicate the three different inversions (the root position is technically an inversion too).

The symbol system not only helps people who cannot read music very well, but also helps any keyboard musician become more creative by encouraging pattern-based thinking and developing the ability to 'see the music in the keyboard.'

You will see these symbols in the illustrations in the modules, and the system is fully explained in the text. You will also find them in the Musicarta Keyboard Chord Generator PDF file included in the Other Resources folder in your download.

☐ Print the two-page file out and have it at hand to refer to.

Musicarta's Key Chords work starts in the all-white-piano-key key of C major, but from Module Seven on, the lesson series requires that you know other, relatively simple, keys as well.

Also included in your Other Resources folder is the Musicarta Key-Specific Keyboards PDF, which shows which keys on the piano keyboard you are to use once the music has a key signature (the collection of sharps or flats at the start of each line of music).

☐ Print the two-page file out and have it at hand to refer to.

Practicing

Everybody recognizes that a certain number of hours' practice time is required to acquire advanced skills. Often, many repetitions will be required to get a riff right, and when you come to play it again, you may feel like you're 'starting from scratch'.

Have realistic expectations! Practice efficiently and revisit recently learned material to 'bed it in'. Enjoy all your intermediate accomplishments, and be a sympathetic teacher.

Understanding Key Chords

Keys, scales and chords

The chords in a song or piece of music aren't random – they come in families called 'keys'. We'll take the key called 'C major' as our example.

Music in the key of C uses mainly the notes of the scale of C major, which can be played using just the white keys of the piano keyboard.

Here is a C major scale – all white keys from C to C, starting on middle C. Note names are given. The numbers are the scale degrees (steps of the scale).

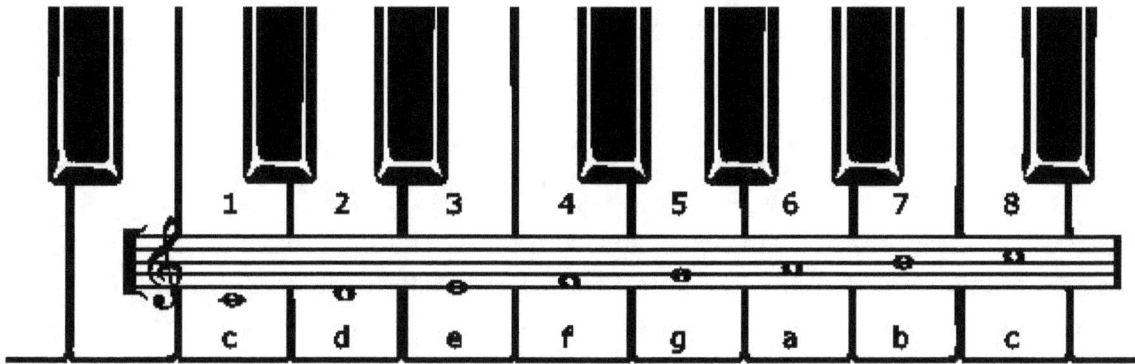

Just the notes:

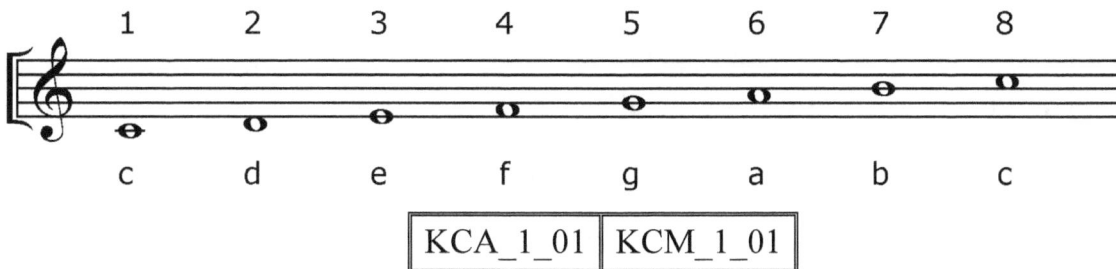

| KCA_1_01 | KCM_1_01 |

(Note that the MIDI file plays the first three musical examples one after another.)

Root position triads

The chords used in a piece 'in C' will chiefly be made of these C major 'scale tones'.

The easiest chords to look at and talk about are those that stack up every other scale tone ('root position triads'). Building these simple chords using just the notes of the scale on each of the scale tones in turn, we find chords of three types – major, minor and diminished.

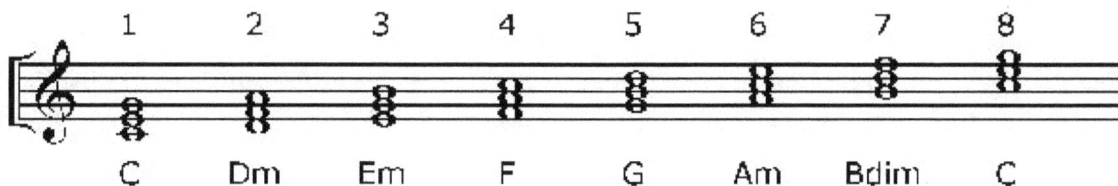

| KCA_1_02 | KCM_1_01 |

Note the chord symbol convention. Capital letters on their own – C, F, G – indicate major chords. To indicate a minor chord, you put a lower-case 'm' after the chord symbol – Dm, Em, Am – and you have to say "minor" – "D minor", and so on. The 'dim' stands for 'diminished' – a third type of triad which we're not concerned with at present.

The chords built on the first, fourth and fifth scale degrees are major chords:

| KCA_1_03 | KCM_1_01 |

A great deal of satisfying music can be made using just these three major chords, and it is these three chords that you are going to learn first. Guitarists routinely learn the I, IV, V (one, four, five) chords as a set and quickly play songs with them. The first part of the Musicarta Key Chords series sets out to make this first and most useful set of key chords as familiar and as easy to find for the keyboard player.

The Roman numeral system of naming chords

If we use Roman numerals to talk about chords, we can use what we learn in any key, and we will be learning about 'chords in general' – harmony – as opposed to just one song or piece.

The system uses Roman numerals to refer to the chords built on the scale degrees.

The system also tells us whether a chord is major or minor. It uses upper case ('capital') numerals to indicate major chords (I, IV, V in the illustration above) and lower case numerals to indicate minor chords (ii, iii and vi).

Working through the Key Chords learning material will teach you to use the Roman numeral system (RNS). To start with, you only need to be able to 'read' the numerals from one to seven and understand the upper case/lower case, major/minor convention. Just be sure to read and say the Roman numerals to yourself whenever you see them.

One (I), Four (IV) and Five (V) – in three places

We have said you are going to learn to play and move between the I, IV and V chords easily. But using only root position I, IV and V chords soon sounds 'clunky'.

(The MIDI file includes the next example as well.)

Now listen to this version of the same chord sequence:

This sounds better because of the smoother top line of the right hand chords, which is achieved by moving not just between the simplest (root position) chords, but to the nearest inversion of the next chord in the chord sequence.

Inversions are formed by taking the bottom note of a triad up an octave to become the new top note. As you work through the Key Chords modules, you will naturally learn about inversions and get better and better at finding them. You do not need to go off and 'learn to play inversions' first, but you can find links to relevant additional musicarta.com learning material at the end of the module.

You now have an explanation of why the Key Chords lesson series concentrates on the three chords mentioned to start with – I, IV and V, or C, F and G major in the key of C major, for instance – and why your first job is learning to find 'nearest inversions' of these chords.

Important notice

The rest of this module presents some more music theory background. Feel free to skip forward to Module Two and start your practical exploration of the key chords right now, if you wish.

Music theory names for the chords

Music theory has yet another set of names for the seven chords you can make from the scale of a key. Like the Roman numerals, they are names for 'chords in any key'.

Here are these music theory names written in the diagram from before:

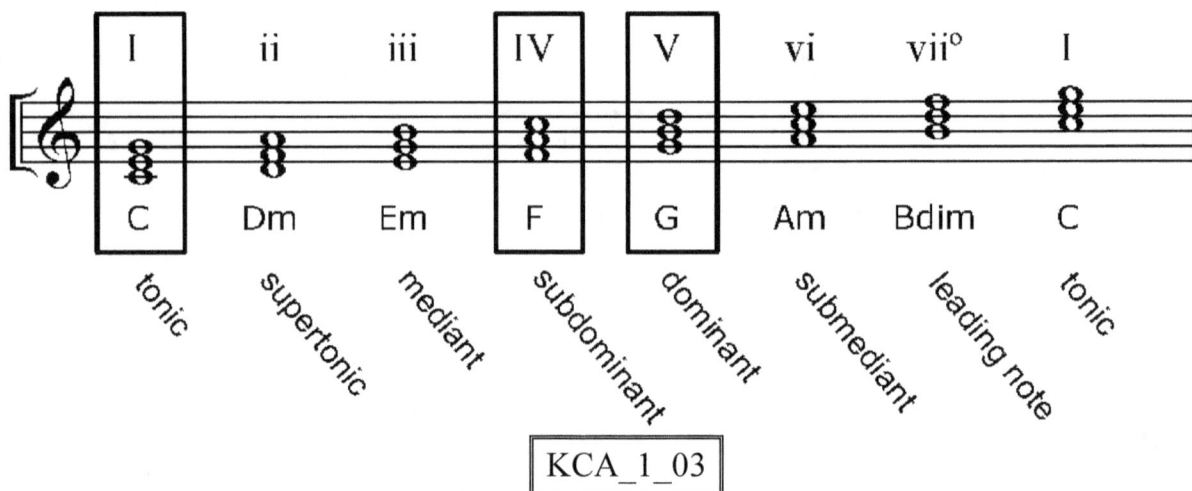

KCA_1_03

Here are the names from tonic (I) to tonic:

RNS*	Music theory	Quality	
I	Tonic	major	(higher)
vii	Leading note	diminished	
vi	Submediant	minor	
V	Dominant	major	
IV	Subdominant	major	
iii	Mediant	minor	
ii	Supertonic	minor	
I	Tonic	major	(lower)

* RNS: Roman numeral system

As with the Roman numerals, you don't have to learn these names by heart in order to progress. At the moment, we're only concerned with the three major chords:

I	IV	V
Tonic	Subdominant	Dominant

These three chords will be referred to sometimes by their RNS names, sometimes by their music theory names, so you will easily get to know both sets of names over time.

This re-arranged diagram might also help you remember the chord names. The tonic (home chord) is now in the middle.

RNS	Music theory	Quality	
V	Dominant	major	(higher)
IV	Subdominant	major	
iii	Mediant	minor	
ii	Supertonic	minor	
I	Tonic	major	
vii	Leading note	diminished	
vi	Submediant	minor	
V	Dominant	major	
IV	Subdominant	major	(lower)

Notice that, counting inclusively from 'one' (the tonic):

The dominant is five steps above the tonic

The subdominant is five steps <u>below</u> the tonic

That is why the subdominant is so called – it's as far below ('sub') the tonic as the dominant is above it – not because it's just below the dominant chord.

The mediant and submediant chords are named the same way:

The mediant is three steps above the tonic

The submediant is three steps <u>below</u> the tonic

In practice, harmony tends to prefer short distances, so chord sequences are more likely to use the closest dominant (V) and subdominant (IV) chords to the tonic – up and down a fourth only (instead of a fifth):

(cont'd)

RNS	Music theory	Quality	
IV	Subdominant	major	(higher)
iii	Mediant	minor	
ii	Supertonic	minor	
I	Tonic	major	
vii	Leading note	diminished	
vi	Submediant	minor	
V	Dominant	major	(lower)

Now the 'sub'dominant is <u>above</u> the dominant!

Summary

In this module you have been introduced to the three most important chords in any key – the major chords that you can build on the first (I), fourth (IV) and fifth (V) scale degrees.

You have learnt about two sets of names for the chords in a key (besides the simple chord-symbols) – the Roman numeral system (RNS) names and the music theory names.

You have learnt that, in order to play decent-sounding music, you have to use flipped 'inversions' of the basic chords.

In the next module, you will learn to play the first pair of chords – I and IV – in three 'nearest inversion' pairs.

Quick links

If you want to do some focused work on finding and practising inversions, here are some Musicarta website resources that will help.

- Musicarta Finding Inversions module
- Mister Musicarta YouTube Inversions video
- Musicarta Broken Chords exercises page

You can access all these and many more chord-related web pages via the Musicarta Chords section (main site navbar tab) home page.

The First Pair – One and Four (I and IV)

To be able to play popular styles fluently, the modern keyboard player needs to be able to move confidently between all the inversions of chords I, IV and V in the key of a song or piece.

The Musicarta Key Chords lesson series breaks this task down and tackles one pair of chords at a time. The first pair of chords is I and IV – the tonic and subdominant.

I and IV pairs in C major

In C major, chords I and IV (tonic and subdominant) are C and F major.

Finding the chord tones

Here are the chord tones of the C and F major chords, shown on keyboards. Practise finding the chord tones, as in the audio clips. Use both hands and any fingers.

C (I)

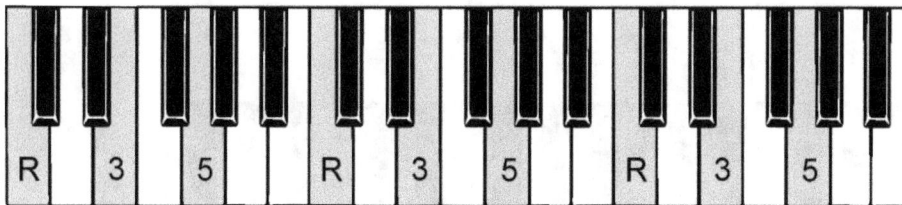

| KCA_2_01 | KCM_2_01 |

F (IV)

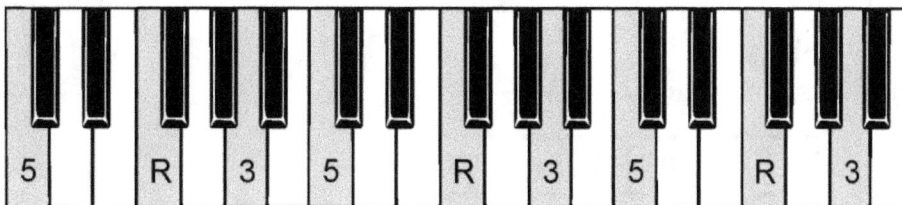

| KCA_2_02 |

The shaded keys on the keyboard are the chord tones. They are labelled R for 'root', 3 for 'third' and 5 for 'fifth' – we will use these indicators later on in the book.

Playing nearest inversions

Starting from a C major root position chord, the 'nearest inversion' of F major we can find is the second inversion chord (shown in the next diagram).

Using your right hand, play

- C major root position
- F major second inversion

- C major root position

…as shown in the keyboards below.

C (I)

F (IV)

C (I)

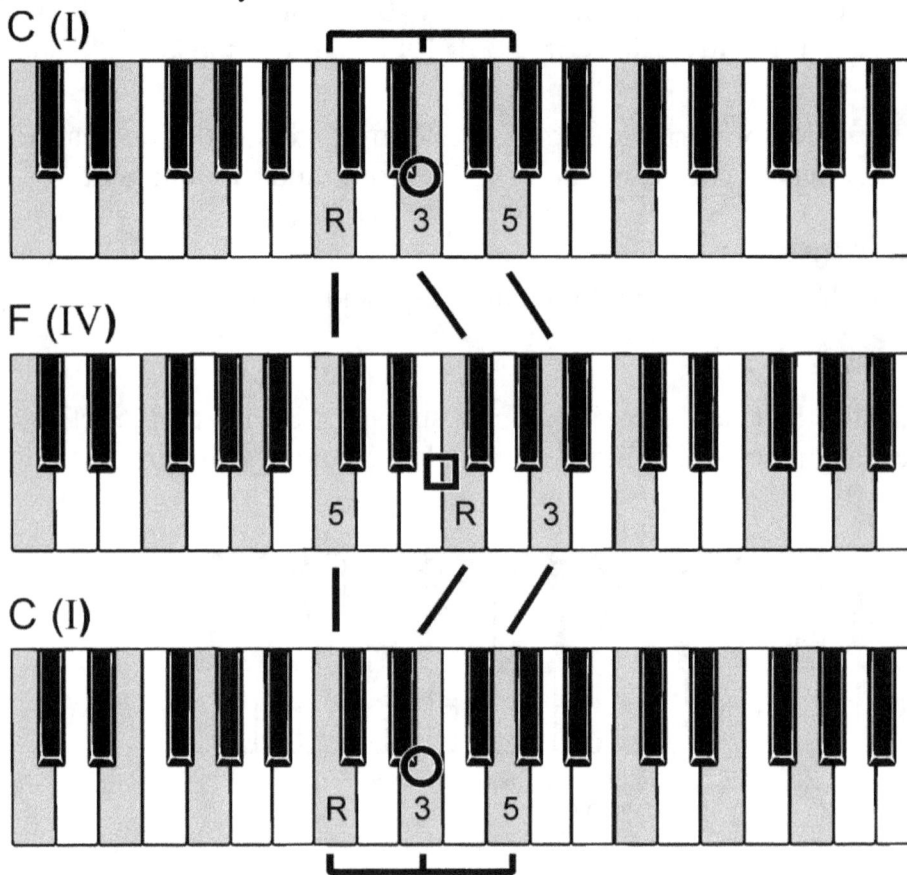

You use the shaded notes with the chord tones R, 3, 5 (root, third, fifth) marked – the ones connected by the lines.

Your performance will sound like this:

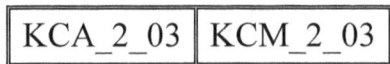

| KCA_2_03 | KCM_2_03 |

Here's the music for that mini chord progression:

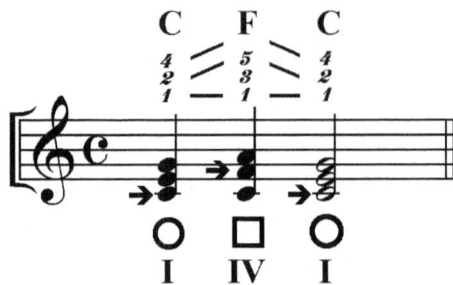

The music has some suggested fingers – 1, 2, 4 then 1, 3, 5 then back to 1, 2, 4. Using the fingering given will help you find notes and keep track of where they go when the chord changes.

The other things you can see in the music are discussed below.

The inversions symbols

In Musicarta teaching material, the three inversions (variants) of the simple triad are indicated so:

a CIRCLE ○ for root position triads, which look like this: (root/name-note arrowed)

a TRIANGLE △ for first inversion triads:

a SQUARE ☐ for second inversion triads:

You don't have to memorise this right now. Over time, you'll find the circle/square/triangle (CST) system of indicating inversions 'sinks in', and makes the inversions a lot easier to find.

The other helpful hint in the music example is the arrows, which point to the roots (name-notes) of the chord. So even if your sight reading isn't good, you can find at least one note quickly and easily – the arrowed note with the same name as the chord.

Voice movement diagrams

The little three-line diagrams between the chord symbols in the diagram represent how the notes in the chords move, and make it easier to learn and remember the performance.

A note in a chord is called a 'voice' – as if a choir was singing the chord – and the three-line graphic is called a voice movement diagram (Musicarta material only). You can see the same movement lines between the three keyboards in the diagram above, but tilted vertically.

| KCA_2_03 | KCM_2_03 |

Voice movement line diagrams help you keep track of where the chord voices go. It's a good idea to say to yourself what the voice movement lines tell you is happening – in this case "The bottom note stays the same; the top two move up then fall back."

Check that you understand this explanation of the voice movement diagrams.

13

The Module One riff

Alternating I and IV chords are common in rock music – you're sure to recognise the sound as soon as we make a riff out of them.

Repeat the three right-hand chords from the above keyboard diagrams, over and over. Add a C bass note before and between the right hand chords. Use the fingering shown in the music. Copy the 'Humpty Dumpty' rhythm from the audio file.

| KCA_2_04 | KCM_2_04 | KC2_DT1 |

More I–IV pairs of nearest inversions

Next, find the nearest inversion of F from the C first inversion chord.

Check yourself against the audio file. Check the suggested fingering in the written-out music:

| KCA_2_05 | KCM_2_05 |

You can play the module riff pattern with this pair of chords also:

| KCA_2_06 B | KCM_2_06 |

Next, find the inversion of F that's nearest to the second inversion C chord. Here's the music manuscript (the keyboard illustration is on the next page).

| KCA_2_07 | KCA_2_07 |

| KCA_2_08 | KCM_2_08 |

Play this pair of chords in the riff rhythm – they sound better an octave lower, around middle C (second audio/MIDI table, above).

Rehearse all three pairs of chords

Here are all three pairs of nearest inversions in music manuscript:

| KCA_2_09 | KCA_2_09 |

Play them over and over until you can see the sound of the chords in the keyboard – until you know what the next chord you're going to play sounds like.

The complete riff

Here are all three pairs of chords in the riff rhythm. You play the first pair twice, then the middle pair twice, then the last pair (at the top for this riff), then the middle pair again.

| KCA_2_10 | KCM_2_10 | KC2_DT1 |

The written-out music is just below but try to work as much as possible from the audio clips, MIDI files, the three C–F–C keyboard illustrations and from memory.

This is the end of the essential I–IV module chord-pair work.

You may be a keyboard player with some years experience, and perhaps be able to read music well. Some optional extra material follows which puts your new chords skills to creative use – you might like to work through it and see how much music just these three pairs of two chords can generate.

You can go however straight on to the Module Three and learn the next pair of key chords – I and V (C and G). You will be prompted to come back and catch up with all the extra material later on, in any case.

Optional extra Module Two material

Important notice

Beginners should approach this optional extra material with caution. If you find the material confusing, just go on to the next module – you will be invited to come back later anyway, when you have more experience, as part of consolidating your knowledge.

Triads as shapes

If we take the music stave (lines) away from the chord-pair music manuscript examples, you can see the chords shapes more clearly – both the gaps within the chords and the movement between them:

Notice that there aren't any chord symbols either. These triads could be anywhere – which frees you to try the patterns in other places on the keyboard.

First variation

If you play three pairs of nearest inversion with G–C–G as the arrowed notes (roots) you will also get a major sound, just like C–F–C, but in the key of G. You can re-run the whole lesson in G.

(This is called 'transposing', and is considered an advanced musical accomplishment!)

The audio clip plays you the three pairs of I-IV chords in G – find those first, then add the rhythm. The MIDI clip on MidiPiano will show you exactly which keys to play.

| KCA_2_11 | KCM_2_11 | KC2_DT1 |

Combine the two sets of chords

Once you can play the I-IV-I pairs in G, combine them with I-IV-I pairs in C. The 'underlying' chord sequence for the riff is this:

G	G	C	G	C	G	C	G

But for each of those chord symbols, you play three chords (I-IV-I) – so the right hand chords you actually play are:

G-C-G	G-C-G	C-F-C	G-C-G	C-F-C	G-C-G	C-F-C	G-C-G

| KCA_2_12 | KCM_2_12 | KC2_DT1 |

More variations

If you play the pattern on roots E–A–E or on A–D–A you will be playing all minor chords, and in RNS notation, the chords will be i-iv-i (minor tonic and subdominant).

The audio clip is in E minor – start on the E minor root position (circle shape) chord.

| KCA_2_13 | KCM_2_13 | KC2_DT2 |

In this riff, you break the chords up – after playing the E minor chord, you play the three chord tones bottom-middle-top one after the other. Watch the MIDI file on MidiPiano for clarification. You can apply that technique to any of the previous riff material in the module.

A D minor (Dorian mode) version

Roots D–G–D give a nice mixed major-minor sound – the tonic (i) is minor, while chord IV (the subdominant) is major. Rehearse the chords first.

KCA_2_14 | KCM_2_14 | KC2_DT3

(Note: This riff ignores the 'nearest inversion' rule on the way down from the top D minor chord.)

The Second Pair – One and Five (I and V)

The modern keyboard player needs to be able to move confidently between the inversions of I, IV and V chords in the key of the relevant song or piece. In Key Chords Module Two, you learnt the 'closest inversion' pairs of chords I and IV (One and Four). In this module, you learn the I and V (Five) pairs in a similar way.

I and V pairs in C major

In C major, the new chord V (Five) is G major.

Finding the chord tones

Here are the chord tones of the C and G, shown on keyboards. Make sure you can find the chord tones, as in the audio and MIDI files. (The audio and MIDI files cover both chords/keyboards.)

C (I)

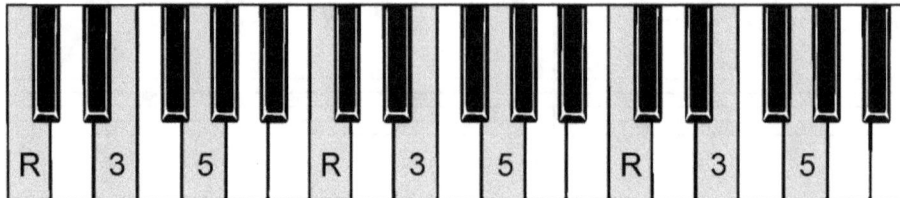

G (V)

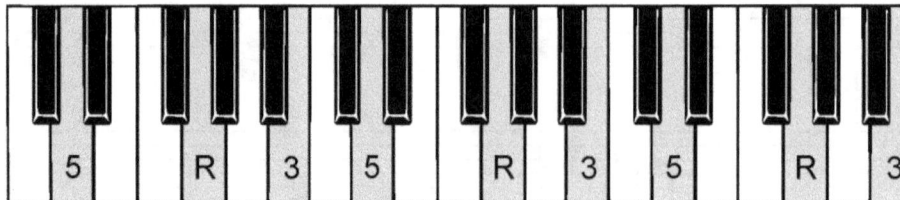

| KCA_3_01 | KCM_3_01 |

Playing the nearest inversions

Just as for chords I and IV, three close-together pairs of I and V chords can be found.

Starting from a C major root position chord, the nearest inversion of G major we can find is the second inversion chord (shown in the next diagram).

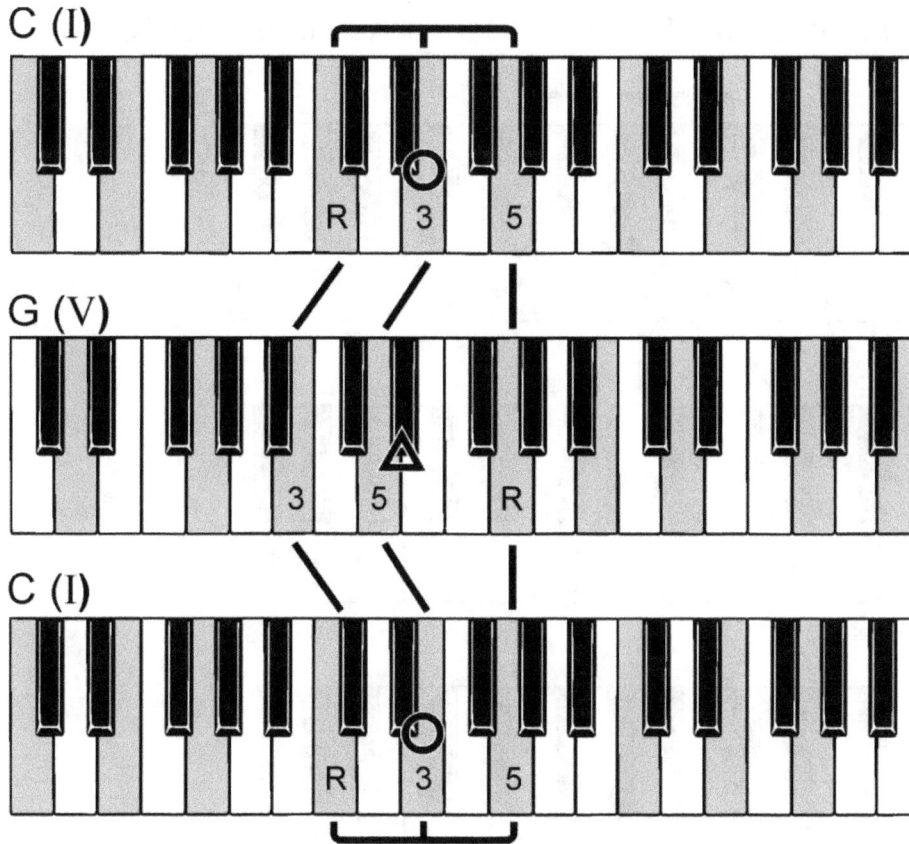

C (I)

G (V)

C (I)

You will sound something like this:

| KCA_3_02 | KCA_3_02 |

This is the written-out music:

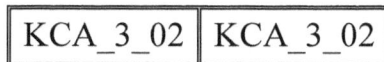

Say out loud what the voice movement diagrams tell you: "The top note stays the same, the bottom two notes step down then back."

Next, start from the C first inversion chord and find the nearest inversion of G.

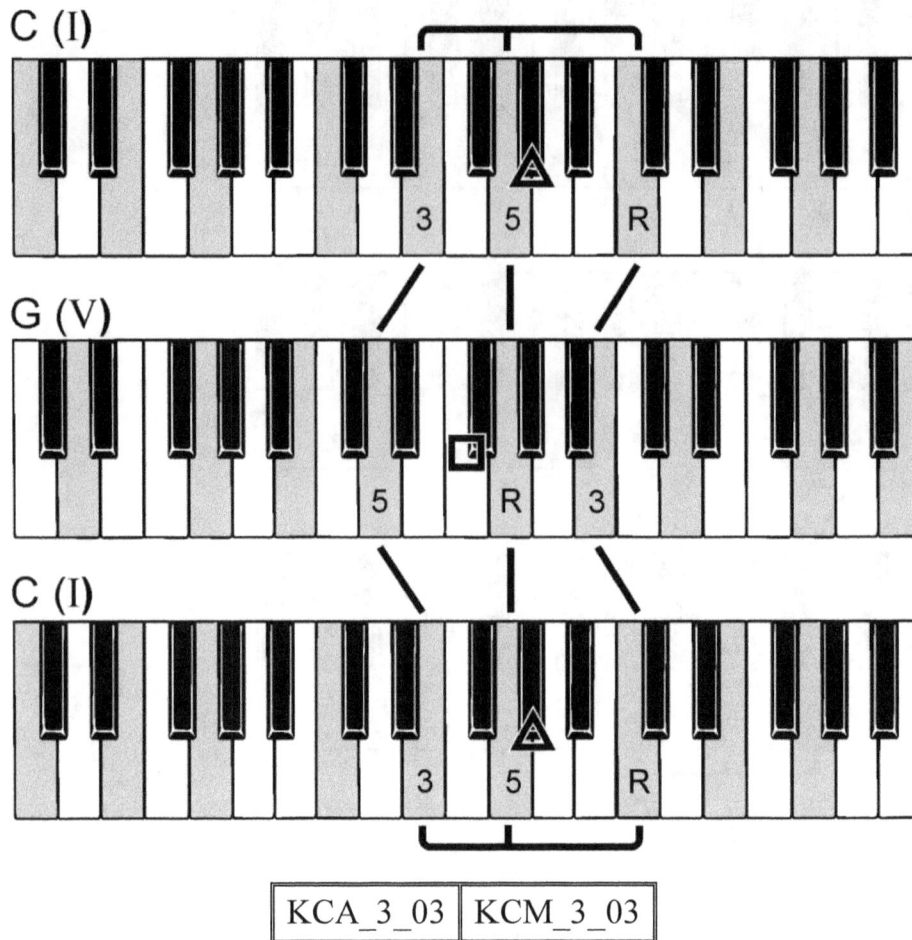

C (I)

G (V)

C (I)

| KCA_3_03 | KCM_3_03 |

Here's the MS:

The voice movement diagrams tell you: The middle note stays the same; the outside notes go down then up again.

The third pair starts from the C major second inversion chord:

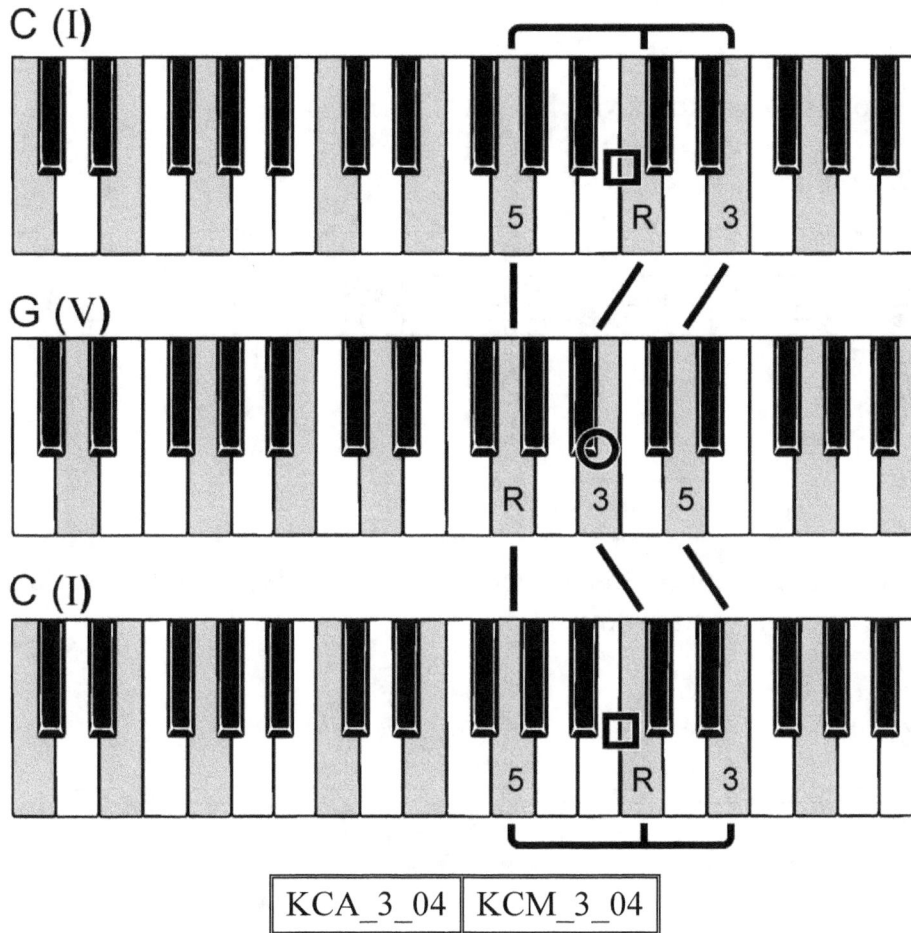

Here's the written-out music:

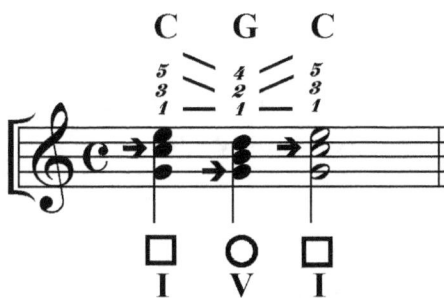

The voice movement diagrams say: The bottom note stays the same; the top two notes move down a step then back up.

Building a riff on I and V

Step 1

Here are the three pairs of I and V chords you have just found:

| KCA_3_05 | KCM_3_05 |

But we will get a much better riff out of this particular material if we re-order the pairs and start from C first inversion an octave lower.

| KCA_3_06 | KCM_3_06 |

The first two pairs of chords in the riff are being played an octave below where you learned them. Check that you are matching the audio file before going on.

Step 2

Play each pair twice. Add a crotchet C 'pedal bass' left hand note. (A 'pedal bass' is one that sticks to the same note no matter what chords are being played above it.)

KCA_3_07 | KCM_3_07

Be sure you can do this confidently. You will need to be sure of the notes once you start the syncopation (next step). Notice how the fingering makes the chord changes easier.

Step 3

Next, practice this rhythmic trick:

KCA_3_08 | KCM_3_08 | KC3_DT1

The chords have doubled up to quavers, two to a beat, but there's only one G chord and the C chord from crotchet beat 3 comes a quaver early.

You see that if are not sure of your chords, playing them 'off the beat' (syncopated) is difficult. Loop the audio file in Audacity or play the MIDI file in MidiPiano with 'Repeat' set for a play-along track.

Together, left, right analysis

The letters T, L, R between the bass and treble clefs in the MS example above stand for together, left and right.

When the rhythm of music gets more complicated – when it is syncopated and one hand or the other is playing off the beat – it pays to be very clear in your mind which hand or hands are playing and in what order. This is what Musicarta calls 'together, left, right analysis' (TLR analysis).

Playing the piano in the modern popular style is a lot more like playing the drums than we realise, and analysing and tapping out the rhythm of syncopated music is a very efficient use of your practice time.

Without music notes, the rhythm of our syncopated riff is this:

KCA_3_09

If we just look at the 'events' in the new syncopated riff – what actually happens, in what order – we find this:

This is a 'beat map'. It shows what beats the right hand (upper notes, stems up) and the left hand (lower notes, stems down) play on. Read it as you listen to the previous audio clip to make sure you can see how it displays the rhythm properly.

The 'sequence of events' is:

T R T R L L

"The hands play together (T), then just the right hand (R), then together again (T), then… (etc.)"

We call it a 'sequence of events' – rather than a rhythm – because to start with we allow ourselves to forget about keeping time altogether until we can tap out (hands on your desk):

T R T R L L

together, right, together, right, left, left

repeatedly.

KCA_3_10

Once you can reliably tap out the 'sequence of events' you can try speeding up and making your left hand taps regular until you're copying the audio clip:

| KCA_3_08 | KCM_3_08 |

You will also find that saying the rhythm out loud helps. The crotchet beats 1, 2, 3, 4 have to come as regular as telegraph poles or railway sleepers. The quaver 'ands' (&) come half way between them without disturbing the rhythm of the main number (1, 2, 3, 4) beats.

Say "One and two and three, four, one and two and three, four…" over the riff audio. Remember:

"If you can say, you can play it!"

Step 4

Now try to apply the rhythm to all the pairs of chords in the riff.

Here are the pairs of chords written out, followed by the rhythm beat map and the relevant audio file. Remember, you play each pair of chords twice.

| KCA_3_11 | KCM_3_11 | KC3_DT1 |

There is written-out music at the end of the module, but playing the riff from these 'How to assemble' instructions is a much more creative achievement.

Step 5 (optional)

Bring the G chord forward a quaver as well:

| KCA_3_12 | KCM_3_12 |

The audio file plays just the first pair of chords, at practice speed. Join in and take over as the clip fades.

Here is the TLR analysis of the new rhythm:

| KCA_3_13 |

There is another tied note. Instead of

T R T R L L

…we now have

T R L R L L

"Spot the difference!"

Use the TRL analysis to practise tapping the new rhythm, as you did before. Say the rhythm out loud as you tap, if you can.

Now apply that rhythm to the other pairs of chords in the riff. Your performance will sound like this:

| KCA_3_14 | KCM_3_14 |

Step 6 (optional)

Try one more version with one bar of one rhythm and then one bar of the other. Add a 'kick' to the bass with notes g and a. This example shows how this two-bar pattern is tapped and counted, and what it looks like in written music.

Apply that to the four pairs of chords for your completed riff.

| KCA_3_15 | KCM_3_15 |

Using music wisely

In the long run, creative musicians play patterns brought to life through the individual notes, so when you see the full MS of a module riff (as on the next page), try not to let your attention be totally dominated by 'the dots'.

The music is only there as a reminder of what the actual notes are. Remember the patterns you learnt it in the build-up – you're playing four pairs of 'closest inversions' twice with a certain rhythm attached. Try to let the circle/square/triangle mark-up and the voice movement diagrams help you find the notes.

This is the end of the essential Module Three material. You can go straight from here to Module Four, where you combine this module's I and V pairs with the I and IV pairs of Module Two and discover what a powerful ability it is to be able to find these chords in all their inversions quickly and surely.

But as before, you can also make lots more music with the keyboard patterns you've learned, so feel free to explore the 'optional extra' riffs which follow. The extra practice will definitely pay off, and, if you find yourself getting discouraged, you can always put it aside and move on with the mainstream module work thread.

Optional extra Module Three material

You can play the I–V module keyboard patterns in the key of F using only the white keys and still get a proper I–V–I chord sequence. The hand shapes will be just the same, but the roots (R) will be F and C instead of C and G.

Here are keyboards showing the closest I and V inversions in F. The chords could be anywhere – high or low – on the keyboard.

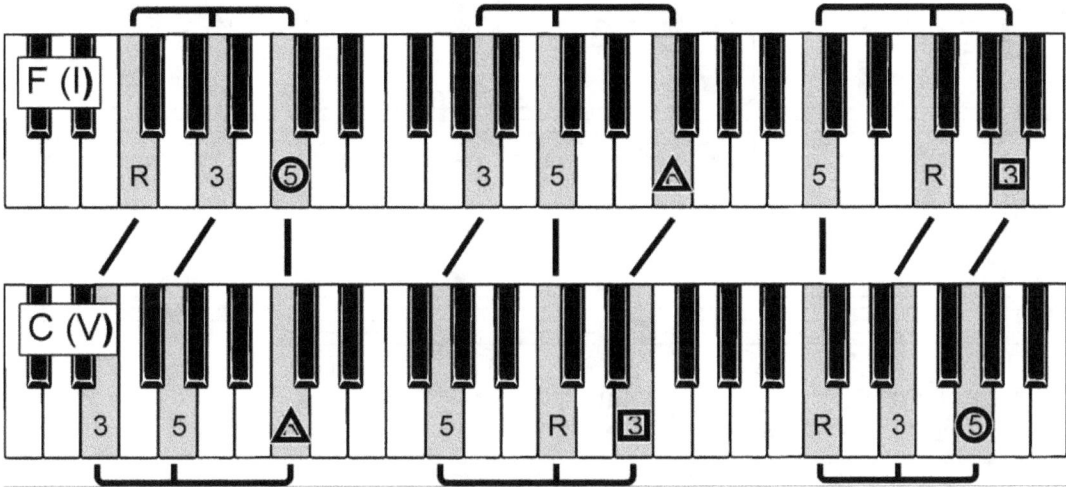

Here are the pairs of chords you're looking for, and a developed riff in F.

| KCA_3_16 | KCM_3_16 |

- The audio/MIDI start out with 'find the pairs' music.
- There is now only one bar of each pair of nearest I–V–I inversions before you move up to the next pair. There is one bar of T R L R L L rhythm, then one of T R T R L L (see the counting in the actual music).
- On the second run-through, there's a 'broken chord' on the way to the next pair of inversions. You climb up the bottom, middle, top (B, M, T) notes of the chord before jumping up an inversion.

Here's some 'skeleton' practice music. Always rehearse your chords first! See if you can play the riff from just this and the full riff audio (KCA_3_16).

Audio/MIDI reference for previous page:

KCA_3_17	KCM_3_17

KCA_3_16	KCM_3_16	KC3_DT2

Combining the two positions

Once you can play the three pairs of closest inversions in F, you can combine the new material with the main module riff to create this advanced inversion study.

KCA_3_18 | KCM_3_18

If you're a non-reader, try to play by ear, using the CST (circle, square, triangle) mark-up and the combined keyboards diagram below to find the inversions.

Here are combined keyboards for C, F and G. The tonic (I/C) is in the middle. The chords can be anywhere, high or low, on your keyboard – only the voice movement lines really count.

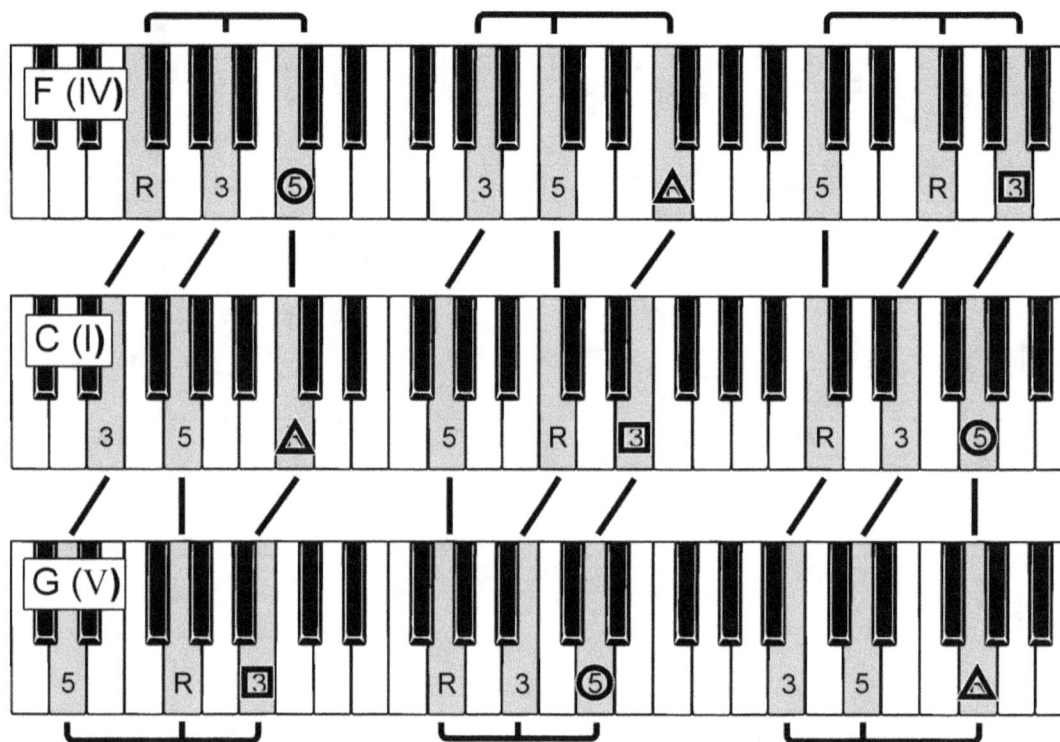

Always 'block the chords out' first, without any rhythm or left hand accompaniment. Here's a MIDI file of what your 'blocking out' might sound like:

KCM_3_19

Pay attention to fingering. Work out what lets you get to that next chord on time, and pencil it in on your hard copy. Note that this is an advanced chord work-out; expect to practice sections only, slower than the audio, to start with.

Practice smart, practice less!

If you read music, it's not efficient to learn a chord study like this note by note from the start to the finish. You learn the music a lot more thoroughly and creatively if you try to get an 'aerial view' first.

Study the music and the audio file repeatedly until you can 'hear' these pattern elements.

- You go up the pairs of C and G chord inversions and come down the pairs of F and C chord inversions.

- There's a 'broken chord' on the way to the next pair. You climb up the bottom, middle and top notes in the chord to go up and come down the top, middle, bottom notes.

Harmonising with I, IV and V

Chords I, IV and V in a chord progression

The Musicarta Key Chords modules so far have shown you how to move easily between chords I and IV (C and F) and I and V (C and G) in the key of C. In this module, you put the three chords together.

We make things a little easier to start with by going through the 'home' I chord every time, and leave moving directly between IV and V, which is more difficult, to the next module.

The module chord sequence is:

$$I–IV–I–V–I$$

…which, in the key of C, is: C–F–C–G–C

The first group of chords

Here is the first set of chords. Notice that they are not simply played top to bottom as before – see the explanation that follows.

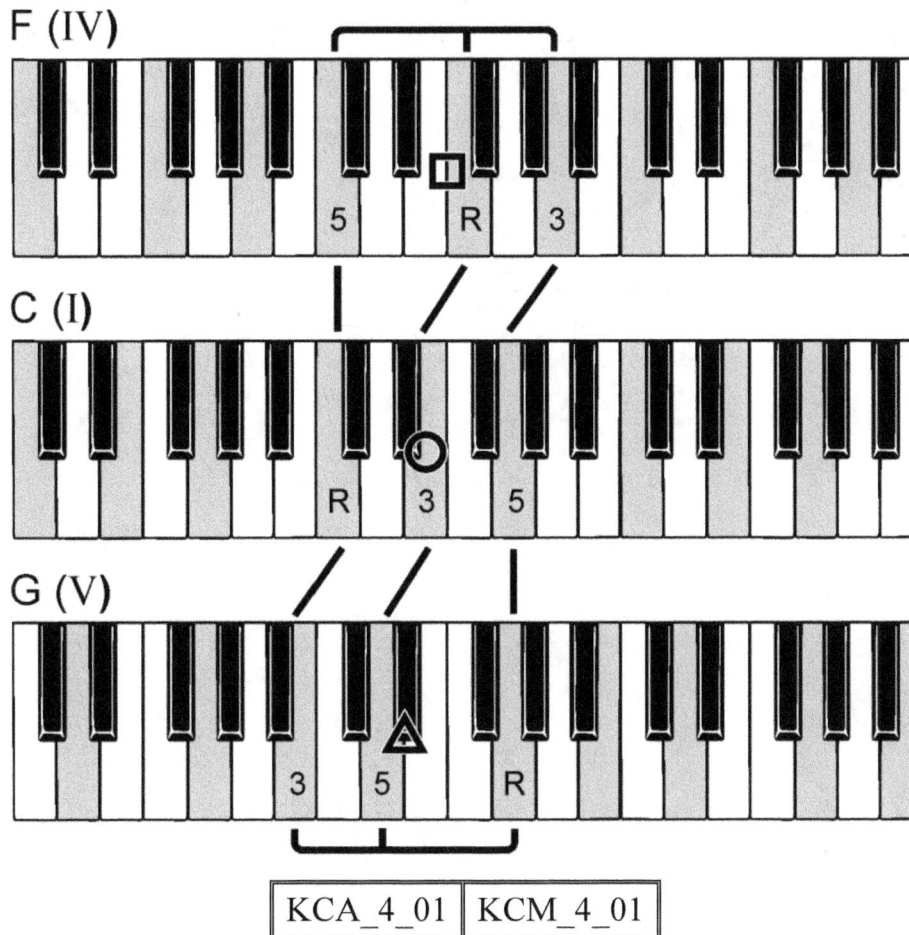

To get the five chords of our mini chord progression out just three keyboards, you read the keyboards like this:

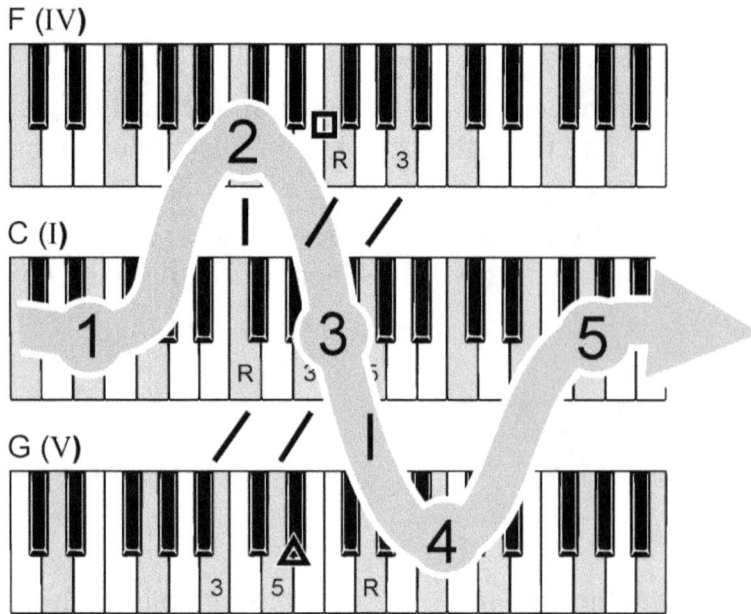

Play the C root position (circle symbol) chord from the middle keyboard, then the F chord from the top keyboard, then the C chord again, then the G chord from the bottom keyboard, then the C chord one last time.

In the left hand, play the roots C, F and G as bass notes, but to add a little spice, play a bass note G under the second C chord:

The 'slash chord'

Playing a chord with a note that's not the root (name-note) in the left hand gives what is called (in popular music) a 'slash chord'. The bass note is usually one of the other chord tones – the third or the fifth.

Our slash chord is indicated C/G. Read the chord symbol as "C over G", or "C with G in the bass." The first letter indicates the chord, the second letter the single bass note.

The second group of inversions

Find the next set of three closest-inversion I, IV and V chords, from C first inversion (triangle symbol). Remember, your chord sequence is still C, F, C/G, G, C. Play the keyboards middle, top, middle, bottom, middle as before.

The third group of inversions

Here is the last group of inversions, from the C second inversion (square symbol).

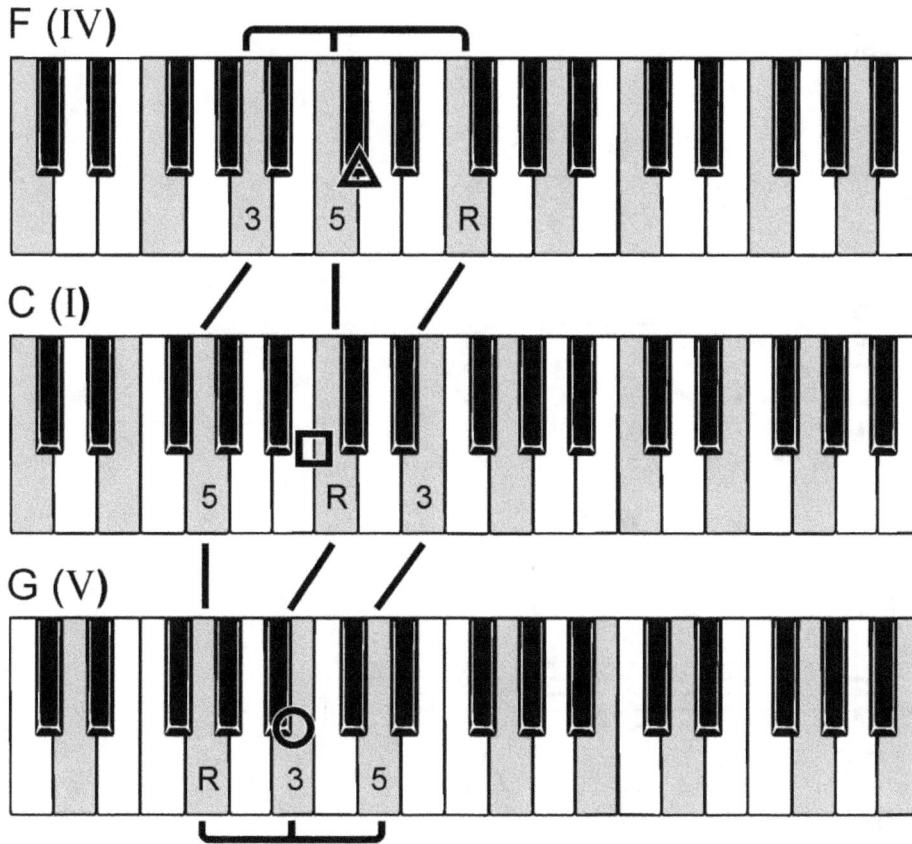

Play it over and over using the fingering given. Study the voice movement lines so you keep track of where the 'voices' go. Knowing which note stays the same is really helpful – but it changes with each different group of inversions.

The groups of inversions combined

KCA_4_05 | KCM_4_05

For our module riffs, we want the option of playing the second and third groups of inversions an octave lower.

Here is how the second and third groups of inversions look written an octave lower. The middle one (from C second inversion) is shown written in both the treble and bass clefs. The one stating from C first inversion (triangle symbol) has to be written in the bass clef.

KCA_4_06 | KCM_4_06

Play the three groups of inversions cycling down from C root position. (The from-second-inversion group only plays once in the audio, although it's written out twice.)

Continue working on your leger-line reading. Keyboard players play a lot around middle C – just where the staves split into bass and treble – so you'll want to be able to read leger lines well. Study the flashcards that came with your download often.

Introducing the Module Four riffs

Musicians-in-training should consciously work on their ability to 'get into a groove' and be carried away by their own playing. This module's chord sequence lends itself perfectly to both African jazz and gospel – both of which offer a great opportunity to do just that.

The Afro-jazz riffs are offered first; the gospel-feel material starts on page 63.

The I–IV–I–V–I mini chord sequence – and particularly the third, slash chord – is typical of South African 'Cape jazz' style, (search Dollar Brand/Abdullah Ibrahim, Basil Coetzee and Hugh Masekela on the Internet and YouTube for examples). The simple three-chord harmony and catchy loping rhythm make for great grooves and lay a good foundation for developing improvisation skills.

There are a total of seven riffs, each divided into practice sections. Read and listen through the complete riffs first, then work through the build-up sections. A short description, together with the audio and MIDI file reference numbers, is given underneath each section.

Use MidiPiano to play the section MIDI files with the Repeat and Piano Roll functions on. You see-and-hear the build-up, and you can slow the performance down too.

The riff beat maps

The Module Four riffs combine the opportunity to practise the I, IV and V chords with 'build-up of syncopation' material for methodically increasing your ability to play syncopated keyboard patterns.

Modern keyboard styles are very syncopated and dedicated practice for these skills is needed. Don't neglect the preparatory chord work, though – you need to know the 'underlying chords' well to syncopate the hands successfully.

There are dedicated beat maps for tricky sections of the riffs, indicated (BM) in the tables where applicable. The beat maps have audio tracks. Loop the audio in Audacity, then read-and-listen until you can hear which drum sounds denote 'right' and 'left', then try tapping along.

The beat maps also indicate an optional (but recommended) crotchet foot-tap. This may seem like an impossibility at first, but practically anything is achievable with practice.

Important note

This module contains a great deal of material, and you don't need to work through all of it before you go on to Module Five. You can skip forward as soon as the chords are 'just coming', and come back at leisure to continue building your skills and repertoire.

Module Four, Riff 1: Anticipate chords and add a bass line

The whole-riff audio/MIDI reference is: KCA_4_07 | KCM_4_07

1. Play your four chords with the bass line, including the 'slash' bass note.

KCA_4_08 | KCM_4_08

2. Bring the second and fourth chord forward a quaver.

KCA_4_09 | KCM_4_09

3. Add four-note bass-line runs – C up to F and G up to C. (See beat map/BM.)

KCA_4_10 | KCM_4_10

4. Anticipate second bar bass note plus one bass note dropped. (BM)

KCA_4_11 | KCM_4_11

5. Optional tweak in the first bar – off-beat RH chord and a missing bass note. (BM)

KCA_4_12 | KCM_4_12

6. Warm-down (and optional simple version).

KCA_4_13 | KCM_4_13

45

Here is the beat map for sections 3, 4 and 5:

KCA_4_14

Module Four, Riff 2: Breaking up the chords and anticipation

The whole-riff audio/MIDI reference is:

KCA_4_15	KCM_4_15

1. Play your four chord with the bass line including the 'slash' bass note:

KCA_4_16	KCM_4_16

2. Play the chords and then break them up bottom, middle, top (BMT).

KCA_4_17	KCM_4_17

3. Anticipate the second and fourth chords – they move into the space of the 'T' (top) quaver of the previous chord.

| KCA_4_18 | KCM_4_18 | BM |

4. This is the next set of inversions down – note the RH is written in the bass clef.

| KCA_4_19 | KCM_4_19 |

5. Do the same break-up-and-anticipate trick with the new set of inversions.

| KCA_4_20 | KCM_4_20 |

6. Wild-card 'teach yourself' riff – use count and TLR to get it.

| KCA_4_21 | KCM_4_21 | BM |

Here is the beat map and audio tap-along track for sections 3 and 6.

| KCA_4_22 |

Module Four, Riff Three: Using inner chord tones as melody notes (Part I)

The next two riffs are slightly different. See if you can pick up the syncopation from just the introductory audio/MS sketch. The music shows the plain chords, then the chord tone that features in the riff – it isn't necessarily the top one.

| KCA_4_23 | KCM_4_23 |

The audio for the whole riff (sections repeat) is: | KCA_4_24 | KCM_4_24 |

1. Starting from the C first inversion chord.

| KCA_4_25 | KCM_4_25 |

2. The chords broken up bottom two voices, top voice.

| KCA_4_26 | KCM_4_26 |

3. Anticipate the 'top voice', and then the final chord too (section doesn't repeat).

| KCA_4_27 | KCM_4_27 |

4. Anticipate across the bar line as well.

| KCA_4_28 | KCM_4_28 |

5. The plain chords, and …

(cont'd)

… the anticipation, rehearsed.

| KCA_4_29 | KCM_4_29 |

6. Develop a bass line under plain minim chords.

| KCA_4_30 | KCM_4_30 |

7. The two hands put together: | KCA_4_31 | KCM_4_31 | BM |

The whole riff: | KCA_4_24 | KCM_4_24 |

The beat map and tap-along audio for section 7 and the completed riff:

KCA_4_32

Module Four, Riff Four: Using inner chord tones as melody notes (Part II)

Again, see how much of the syncopation you can pick up from just the introductory audio/MS sketch.

| KCA_4_33 | KCM_4_33 |

The whole riff audio/MIDI reference is:

| KCA_4_34 | KCM_4_34 |

Here's the build-up of syncopation:

1. The 'underlying chords' – nearest inversion from C root position.

2. The chords broken up, leaving chord tones over for the second beat.

| KCA_4_35 | KCM_4_35 |

| KCA_4_36 | KCM_4_36 |

3. With anticipation in the first bar.

| KCA_4_37 | KCM_4_37 |

4. Anticipation in the second bar.

| KCA_4_38 | KCM_4_38 |

5. Anticipation in both bars.

| KCA_4_39 | KCM_4_39 | BM |

6. Developed bass line under plain minim chords.

| KCA_4_40 | KCM_4_40 |

7. The two hands put together for the finished riff.

| KCA_4_41 | KCM_4_41 | BM |

The audio/MIDI for the whole riff is:

| KCA_4_34 | KCM_4_34 |

Here's the beat map and audio tap-along for sections 5 and 7:

KCA_4_42

Working well

You will probably need to work through these build-ups several times (that is, on several different occasions) before you have this syncopation 'at your fingertips'.

Use all the tools you have. Play the MIDI segments in MidiPiano on Repeat – slow it down if necessary, and just copy. Play sections on a phantom keyboard on your desk top to get the feel first. Loop the segment audio file in Audacity and play along.

It all depends on your being prepared to keep going until you get it, or to come back and have another go until you do – and then to come back and do it all over again until it's 'just there for you'.

Note also that finding an in-the-meantime groove of your own, not given here, that you can keep going and enjoy, is a point scored. Improvisers' skills are built of many, many little discoveries like that.

Interlude: Beat map round-up

Take a moment to revisit these beat maps.

KCA_4_31

KCA_4_32

You cannot have too much practice tapping out rhythms like these, and it's work you can do anywhere.

Module Four, Riff Five: Jumping between positions

In the Key Chords material, you first learn sets of 'nearest inversions', and move in the riffs to the closest inversion for our next chord. But at some point, you are going to want to step out of the 'nearest-inversion-only' constraint to move more freely up and down the keyboard. This next riff uses the Module Four Afro-jazz I–IV–I–V–I chord sequence but swaps between inversion groups 'midstream'

Here's the riff you're going to work up to. Don't try and play from the music unless you're a good sight-reader – just listen to the audio/MIDI material for orientation. It's a long string, but there are lots of great-sounding intermediate steps.

| KCA_4_43 | KCM_4_43 |

There are no written out beat maps for this riff. The audio beat tracks exactly follow the music – read the music as you listen to the beat tracks and tap along.

Now for the build-up of syncopation.

1. Practice the string of chord with the simple minim bass (left hand) notes. The places where the hand jumps between nearest inversion groups are shown with the little double slash mark (//) – check to see you understand.

| KCA_4_44 | KCM_4_44 |

2. Now start listening for melodies using the inside chord tones – like this:

The MIDI file of this section shows the left hand playing the chords and the right hand playing the selected 'melody' chord tones. Don't try to actually play it – it's just to make plain where the melody has come from.

| KCA_4_45 | KCM_4_45 |

3. Now you play the right hand as if it is both a solo line and its own accompaniment. You save chord tones for the second melody note and play the rest. The second F chord even gets pared down to just two notes.

Add the bass line (in the audio) if you want.

| KCA_4_46 | KCM_4_46 |

4. Then – reverting to the simple melody line for now – you add some syncopation. Here's one possibility:

You will need to pay attention to the fingering to get to the notes on time. The beat map is not written out – there are only two places where the

| KCA_4_47 | KCM_4_47 |
| Beat track: KCB_4_47 | |

right and left hands play together (T).

> Note that you can use the MIDI file of any of these sections as tap-along beat map. Play the MIDI file with MidiPiano set to 'Repeat', ignore the actual notes and just tap along, green for the left hand, red for the right.

5. Next, add in whatever chord tones you're not saving for melody notes:

Notice that you get a count (1, &, etc.) when either left or right (or both) happens on that beat, but the crotchet foot tap is not included.

KCA_4_48	KCM_4_48
Beat track: KCB_4_48	

There are two places in this riff (in bars 2 and 4) where the right hand splits into two, playing a melody note and its own 'rhythm section' chords. Follow the MIDI and audio files for some practice with this tricky hand movement.

KCA_4_49	KCM_4_49

You actually play this material in this rhythm:

KCA_4_50	KCM_4_50

6. Now we start developing the bass line. Here's the syncopated bass line under the original minim chords.

Prepare by tapping along with the beat track – with a steady left foot crotchet tap going as well, if you can.

KCA_4_51	KCM_4_51
Beat track: KCB_4_51	

7. You will probably want to put the hands together two bars at a time. Here are the first two bars as a repeating practice segment:

This practice segment is lacking a few 'joining up' notes form the syncopated melody (section 4)

KCA_4_52	KCM_4_52
Beat track: KCB_4_52	

> Study tip: You can slow the MIDI tracks down in MidiPiano until you can tap or play along. Remember, you can settle for an approximation for as long as needs be!
>
> "A bird in the hand is worth two in the bush!"
>
> Work with the groove you <u>can</u> play, even if it's not exactly the one in the audio clip or written down. The one you can play is <u>yours</u>, and any groove you can 'keep coming' is worth much more than a 'better' one you can't get going at all!

8. Here is the second half of the full riff.

Watch out for the tricky 'T L' on beats '& 3' in the first bar.

KCA_4_53	KCM_4_53
Beat track: KCB_4_53	

You just add the joining-up notes in the second bar for the full line.

The music is fully marked up. It isn't really music to read – there's far too much information. (A performance like this wouldn't usually be written down anyway.) It's music for 'unpacking' – a 'blow-by-blow' account.

KCA_4_43	KCA_4_43
Beat track: KCB_4_43	

Try playing sections on an imaginary keyboard on your desktop, concentrating on the TLR (together, left, right) analysis and the counting in turn – practising away from the keyboard is very effective.

Getting creative with the Afro-jazz groove material (Riff Six)

The purpose of working over the possibilities and permutations of a chord sequence so many times is that, at some point, your fingers 'start doing the talking' and you improvise new riffs.

This batch of riffs shows that sort of process in operation. Try to work them out from the audio and MidiPiano performance files before referring to the MS.

Example One

You can easily make a whole riff from just the last two bars of Riff Five. Play the material an octave higher first then drop down with the usual joining run.

| KCA_4_54 | KCM_4_54 |

Notice how the solo improvisation is being built up. You play a four-bar phrase – maybe twice – then you catch your breath just repeating a two-bar phrase before your next 'solo'.

Example Two

You can combine sections in different orders to make 'new' music. Here is Riff 4 with the second half of Riff 5:

KCA_4_55 KCM_4_55

Example Three

| KCA_4_56 | KCM_4_56 |

The F (IV) chord in this style of music often becomes an 'F6' chord. The '6' refers to the sixth scale-tone note above the F – note D. If you take any C major triad one key to the right ('up') and play it over an F bass, you are playing an F6 chord.

Example Four

This 'holding pattern' uses the F6 chord in the Riff Two material, with a slightly different rhythm. Notice how just a very slight difference in the second half stops the music sounding repetitive and gives you a whole new segment.

| KCA_4_57 | KCM_4_57 |

Example Five

This riff moves the C first inversion chord one key to the right to make the F6 chord – then up another step to make a new kind of C/G slash chord.

| KCA_4_58 | KCM_4_58 |

The G7,9 chord is:

- An F6 chord over a G bass…
- Looks like a D minor chord over a G bass…
- Take any C triad up one key (to the right) and play it over a G bass.

The possibilities are endless! Listen out in your head for the tunes and grooves suggesting themselves. Hum vague possibilities and see if you can play them. The old saying, "You can't make an omelette without breaking eggs!" sums it up, so give yourself permission to make a few mistakes – and see if any of them sound any good!

Interlude: Inversions as shapes

Here are the three inversion positions of our I – IV – I – V – I chord sequence 'off the stave'. There are good reasons for considering triads in this way.

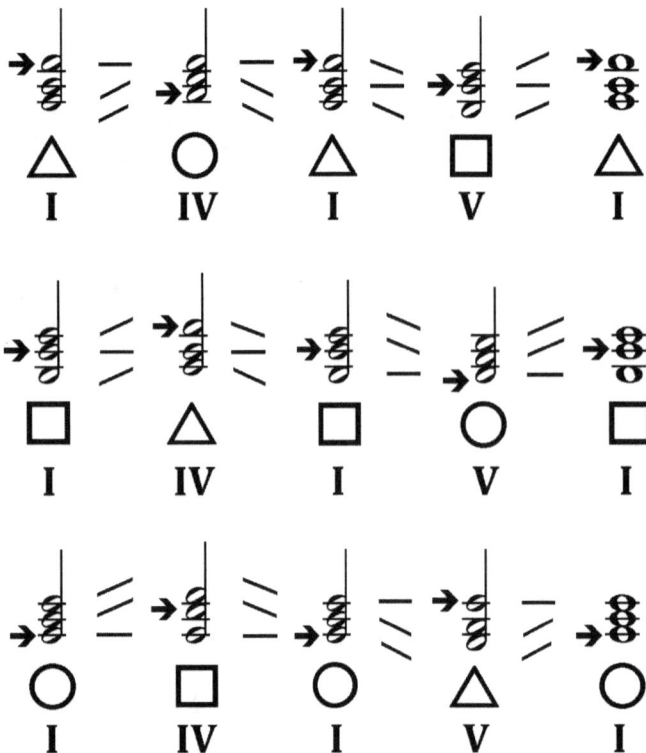

Our simple triads use only scale tones, separated by either one unused scale tone or two. Within a triad, you either play one (a scale tone), then miss one, then play one (P–M–P), or you play one, miss two, and play one (P–M–M–P).

The three inversion of the simple triad combine these two sizes of gap.

Symbol*	Type	In music	Tones and gaps (reading upwards)
○	Root position		P M P M P
△	First inversion		P M P M M **P**
□	Second inversion		P M M **P** M P

* These symbols are used in Musicarta teaching material only. P = play, M = miss.

It's useful to know which of the three chord tones in an inversion is the root (name-note). The root is arrowed in the music and exaggerated in the P–M–P mark-up.

Knowing your triads this way helps your 'educated keyboard guesswork' along a lot.

- If you want to know what right hand triad you are playing, the name-note (root) will <u>probably</u> be the arrowed note (no guarantees!).

- If someone asks you for, say, "an F chord", you can make any of these shapes, using just white keys, with F as the arrowed note and that will give you an F chord. This is true for any C, F or G major chord, and also any D, E and A minor chord – eighteen chords from one simple formula.

- If you're playing a triad you like in the right hand, the arrowed note (root) is the most likely note to play in the left hand (bass). Experimentation is encouraged!

Voice movement diagrams

Using just the white piano keys, you can only play our I–IV–I–V–I triad/voice moment combination with note C as the arrowed note in the I chord (and therefore with F as IV and G as V).

Try it! Example:

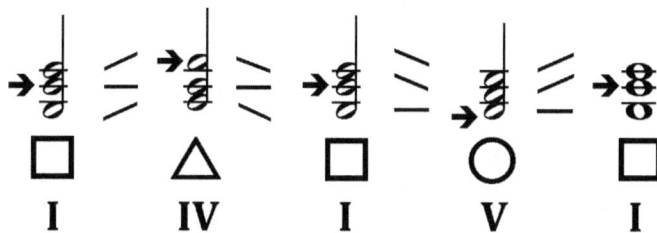

| I | IV | I | V | I |

But voice movement diagrams, individually or in combinations, offer are a great way to start exploring chords more freely.

Here is the full set of voice movement diagrams. Not all the voice movements work from all inversions (and still take you to another proper inversion).

- The voice movements in the top row of the table work best with root position triads
- The second row work best with first inversion triads
- The third row work best with second inversion triads.

(These guidelines shouldn't stop you experimenting. You will find some interesting chords by ignoring them!)

Play a triad and find a left hand bass note using the arrowed note method from the previous table.

Change your triad according to your selected voice movement diagram and find the new chord's root for the bass note. Experiment with black keys to improve the sound, if you think it needs it. Try applying some of the rhythmic textures from this book to your chords.

Module Four, Riff Seven: A gospel-feel I–IV–I–V–I groove

The gospel feel

The gospel-blues feel runs through all R&B (rhythm and blues) popular music, and nearly all great soul singers have had gospel choir training. Any modern musician wanting to play music that speaks to the heart should try to cultivate his or her ability to conjure up some gospel feel. Walking intervals and the module I–IV–I–V–I chord sequence present an excellent opportunity both to work up a groove that carries you along and keeps the notes coming, and to practice your syncopation skills.

KCA_4_59

…demonstrates the kind of performance this section of Module Four aims to guide you towards. (This would be just the start of your own improvisation or composition.)

First, some theory.

Intervals

In music theory an interval refers to the distance between notes, and also means those notes played together.

The most tuneful interval is the third. This is what thirds look like in music:

(…not to play, just to look at!)

You can follow this discussion about tuneful intervals with these audio/MIDI clips. You hear-and-see thirds, sixths and tenths being created, counted, and 'walked' up and down. Try to imitate what you hear – or just copy the MIDI file.

KCA_4_60	KCM_4_60

Intervals are counted inclusively, that is, there's no zero – you start counting from 'one'. What you actually count is scale tones, but if you don't know the scale, you're fairly safe just counting note letter names or lines <u>and</u> spaces on the musical stave.

a third   1 - 2 - 3   C - D - E   line-space-line

You can walk thirds around on the keyboard and they will always sound nice.

If we 'invert' our harmonious third (take the bottom note C up an octave to the top), we get another equally harmonious interval – a sixth.

a third   a sixth   1 - 2 - 3 - 4 - 5 - 6   E - F - G - A - B - C
                          line   line   line
                             space   space   space

The sixth also walks around tunefully.

(For our riff, you will use right hand fingers 1 and 5 for the sixths.)

If we take bottom-note C of our original third down an octave, we get tenths (an octave plus a third). These 'walking tenths' also sound good.

a third   a tenth

You have to use two hands for this exercise.

The chord sequence

The gospel riff chord sequence is still I–IV–I–V–I, but the movement is much more step-wise. Recall the table from Module One (next page). We said at that point that harmony tends to prefer shorter distances, and chord sequences are more likely to use the closest dominant (V) and subdominant (IV) chords.

This is particularly obvious in the I–IV–I–V–I gospel riff. You will be walking the intervals up four steps from the tonic to the IV (subdominant) chord and down four steps to the V (dominant) chord – as you heard in the intervals audio/MIDI clips.

RNS	Music theory	Quality	
IV	Subdominant	major	(higher)
iii	Mediant	minor	
ii	Supertonic	minor	
I	Tonic	major	
vii	Leading note	diminished	
vi	Submediant	minor	
V	Dominant	major	(lower)

Drum tracks for the gospel riff

There are audio drum tracks suited to this gospel-feel material (in a folder called Drums_KC_Gospel Riff) which you can loop in Audacity to give your practice impetus.

> KC4_ gospel_drums_1-6

Experiment with these or find a style in your own preferred rhythm station (drum machine) that works and set the tempo to about 100 bpm for a backing track – or slower to practice.

You can slow down audio drum tracks in Audacity using the playback speed control ringed in the illustration. Ninety percent will give you about 90 bpm – an easy practice speed. You have to click on the green arrow to cue the tempo change.

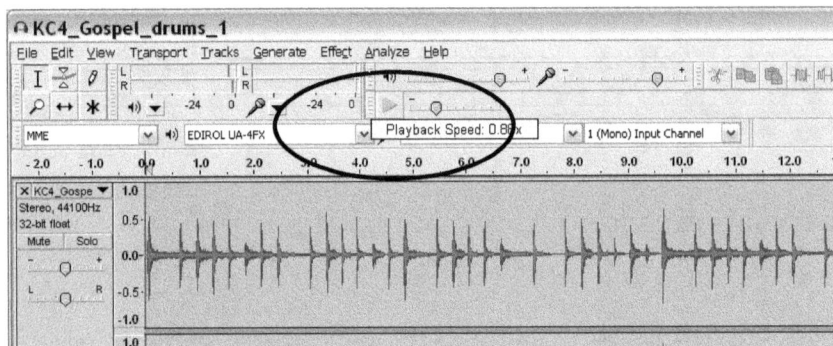

Learning the gospel riff

Learn the first stage movements (without syncopation) thoroughly first.

Use the music manuscript, the audio files and the MIDI files on MidiPiano to help build up the syncopation. Use the MS to formalise your reading and rhythm counting.

Each additional 'degree of syncopation' has a tap-along beat track. At the end of the entire gospel-feel exercise, revise the build-up of syncopation purely as a tapping exercise. The more freedom and variety you have in your hand-patterning, the more interesting your playing will be.

Sixths and tenths, no syncopation

We start with sixths in the right hand, a straight four beats to the bar.

To avoid leger lines as far as possible, the music for the right hand is written in the bass clef. With four bets in a bar, if you set off walking straight away you'll arrive at your new chord a beat early, so we play the first interval twice (or jump to another), then set off. (Composing is full of little 'tweaks' like this, to make things fit.)

| KCA_4_61 | KCM_4_61 |

Here is the basic beat map for the gospel groove – the plain sixths and the tenths below. The count covers only the right hand. Work at keeping the (left) foot going.

KCA_4_62

With the tenths, try to play a third note somewhere. Note the RNS chord names.

KCA_4_63 | KCM_4_63

First degree of syncopation

Start with the sixths.

The count remains the same *(simile)* right up until the last bar.

Here is the beat practice map for the first degree of syncopation. The 'RH' is the moving interval – sixths or tenths. The first half of the beat map demonstrates the first six bars of the riff; the second half (after the double bar line) covers the ending. Practice both separately.

Playing this rhythm in tenths, the third note of the chord is also anticipated – pulled forward over the bar line – so in the end, there's no note on count 1 (just your foot-tap).

| KCA_4_65 | KCM_4_65 |

Second degree of syncopation

The sixths:

| KCA_4_67 | KCM_4_67 |

The tenths:

KCA_4_68   KCM_4_68

Here is the beat map for the second degree of syncopation. Repeat the first two bars of the beat map until the 'ending' – second half of the beat map.

KCA_4_69

The finished riff

The sixths:

KCA_4_70	KCM_4_70

And the tenths:

KCA_4_71 | KCM_4_71

Here is a beat map to rehearse the ends of the two halves of the riff. Practice separately.

KCA_4_72

There is a great deal material in this module. You do not need get through all of it before going on to Module Five and the direct IV–V jump.

The module will repay many return visits. You will probably have settled for a few 'approximations' in the interests of moving forward (as recommended), but all good musicians are continually 'tightening up' the accuracy of their syncopation, building up speed and increasing the number of tricks at their fingertips.

Music that you know as well as this is ideal material for transposing into other keys, too. Set yourself the goal of playing these riffs in D major and B♭ – our two transposing keys – at some stage.

I, IV and V in Three Places

The I–IV–V chord progression

Modules Two and Three in this Key Chords volume explored the basic I–IV–I and I–V–I chord changes and combined them in the Module Four I–IV–I–V–I chord sequence. Module Five explores the other possible movement in this group of chords – direct from IV to V (F to G in key C) – to give the I–IV–V chord sequence.

Finding I–IV–V in the Module Four chord progression

Start from the I-IV-I-V-I Module Four chord progression. To find I–IV–V chord progressions, you just drop the second I chord (we'll drop the final I chord as well). Example:

KCA_5_01	KCM_5_01

…playing just the first, second and fourth chords, becomes

KCA_5_02	KCM_5_02

Note that there's a new voice movement diagram between the F (IV) and G (V) chords:

Three downward-sloping lines – 'Everything moves down'. There are no shared notes between F and G chords, so either everything goes down, or…

…everything goes up. Note that voice movement diagrams only show whether a voice stays the same or moves up or down. The fact that the lines are parallel doesn't mean the chord shape (inversion) stays the same.

Find the three groups of I–IV–V nearest inversions.

First group of inversions

Note: You read/ and play these chords from the top down.

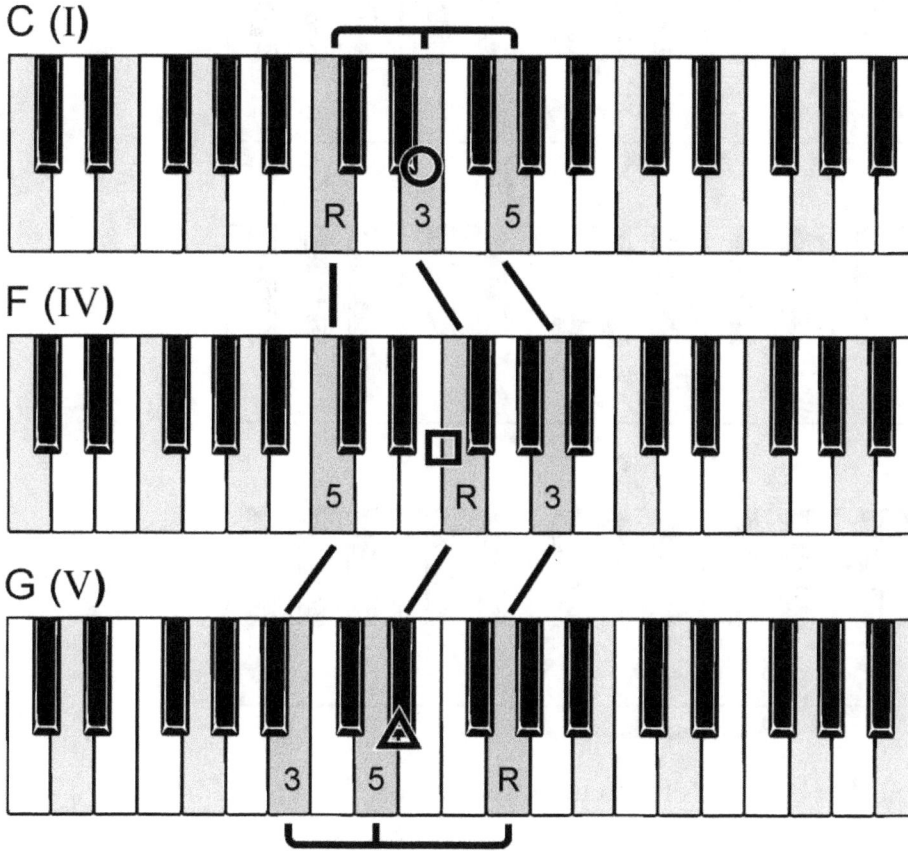

C (I)

F (IV)

G (V)

| KCA_5_02 | KCM_5_02 |

Play a left hand bass note with the right hand chords. Use roots C, F, G.

Second group of inversions

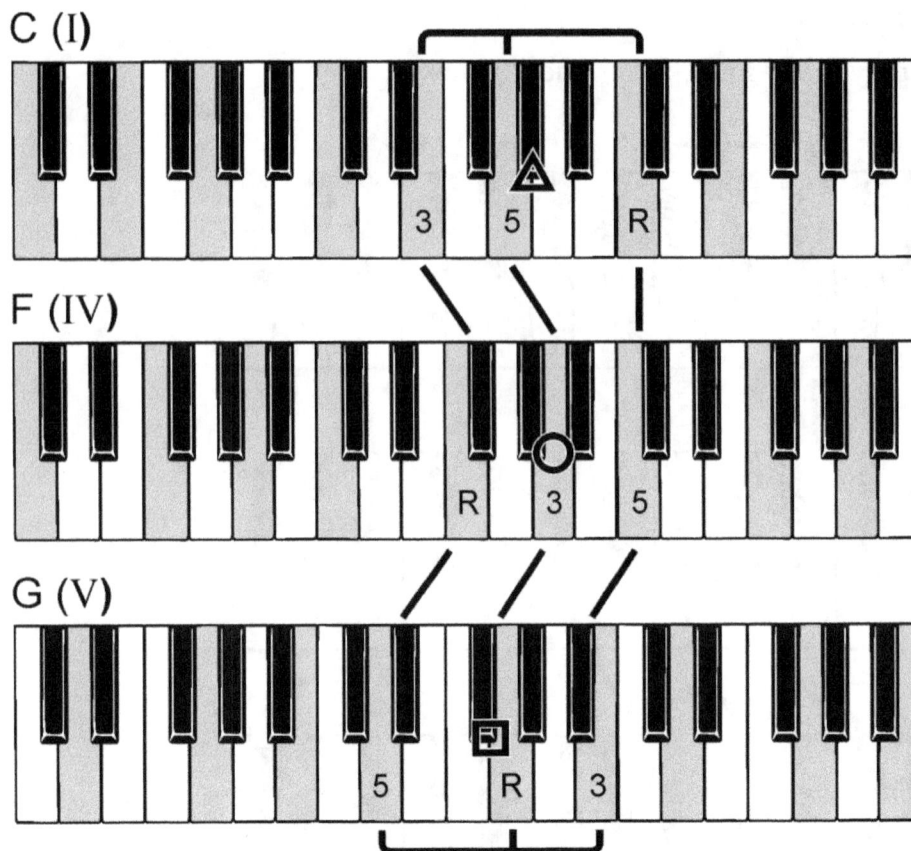

C (I)

F (IV)

G (V)

Find the chords on your keyboard. Refer to the music example below for the best fingering.

| KCA_5_03 | KCM_5_03 |

Third group of inversions

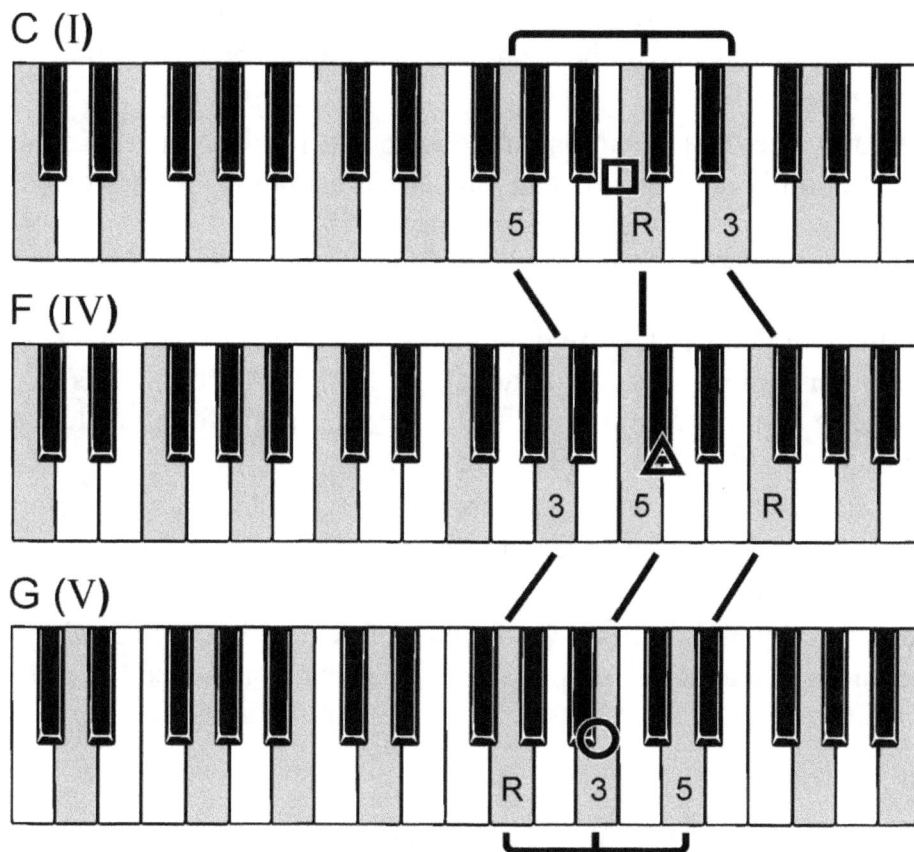

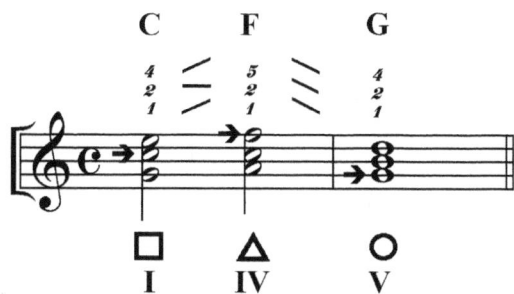

C (I)

F (IV)

G (V)

| KCA_5_04 | KCM_5_04 |

Here are all three sets of inversions played one after the other.

| KCA_5_05 | KCM_5_05 |

Module riff: 'La Bamba'

I–IV–V chord sequences, both quick and slow, form the basis for thousands upon thousands of popular songs. But, as played here, the I–IV–V chord changes fit the famous pop song 'La Bamba' perfectly.

You can find many performances of La Bamba on YouTube* – Richie Valens' version is perhaps the most famous and it's in C, so you can play along using the chords you've learnt.

Drum tracks

The chord changes in the recorded version are quite fast – you will learn and practice much more slowly first. Included in your download is a collection of drum tracks to support your practice and inspire your improvisations. They are in the folder called Drums_KC_Bamba and labelled (for example) DFLB_1_140.

The middle figure (_1_ etc.) is arbitrary and just there to help you identify satisfactory rhythms and speeds. The last figure is the speed in beats per minute (bpm), so you can have some idea of what to expect.

So save space and clutter, individual drum tracks are not referenced in the following tables. Load the drum tracks in Audacity and press shift-spacebar for looped (continuous) playback.

The first I–IV–V performance

Start by working some rhythm into the I–IV–V chord changes.

1. The I–IV–V chords – nearest inversions from C root position.

| KCA_5_06 | KCM_5_06 |

2. Syncopation in the bass line.

| KCA_5_07 | KCM_5_07 |

Here's the beat map/track to work up that syncopated left hand (section 2):

(* Note that Musicarta cannot guarantee the legality of any YouTube content.)

KCA_5_08

Add more rhythmic development:

3. The third right hand chord is pulled forward over the bar line (anticipated)

KCA_5_09 | KCM_5_09

4. The right hand is 'thickened up'.

KCA_5_10 | KCM_5_10

Here's the beat map/track for the new developments (one of each sort)

KCA_5_11

5. Here are sections 3 and 4 joined up and played as a proper line of music:

KCA_5_12 | KCM_5_12

6. Play that line of music using the next group of inversions up:

Everything is just the same except you are using the next set of I–IV–V 'nearest inversions' up.

| KCA_5_13 | KCM_5_13 |

7. The next set of inversions up, but notice the fuller right hand in the second half.

The version in the first two inversion groups is the easy/lazy version – you just repeat the top note of the chord, not the whole thing. Try both versions.

| KCA_5_14 | KCM_5_14 |

8. To finish, repeat the first group of inversions an octave higher.

| KCA_5_15 | KCM_5_15 |

Play all four positions straight through, one after the other, over a drum backing track looped in Audacity or in your own software.

Moving between the groups of inversions

To get the most out of all the inversions you've learned, you need now to start moving **between** the groups of inversions 'midstream', and not just at the end of a group.

We can practise this by moving up to the next group of inversions on the last V chord of a I-IV-V mini sequence.

This time, we'll start on the C (I) second inversion chord. We play the I-IV-V group first, then play it again, but using the V (G) chord from the next group of inversions up to take us up into the next group.

KCA_5_16 | KCM_5_16

The second, higher G chord takes you up smoothly to the next group of inversions. Do the same thing here.

IKCA_5_17 | KCM_5_17

And again:

KCA_5_18 | KCM_5_18

And repeat at the top for a musical finish:

| KCA_5_19 | KCM_5_19 |

Practice until you can play the four lines through without a break. Practice from where you go wrong - don't go back to the beginning every time you make a mistake.

Play the whole string

Here are the 16 bars at practice speed. Play the right hand chords on their own to start with. Keep your eyes scanning ahead and try to join in again with the music if you lose it,

| KCA_5_20 | KCM_5_20 |

You need a firm grasp of the whole rising string of chords before you start adding the syncopation. This represents a considerable achievement on its own!

Syncopate the new chords

Now play all four lines together with the syncopation from before. Here's an example to follow.

> KCA_5_21 | KCM_5_21

Here's sample MS and the beat map for the first phrase of the audio track. Use the skeleton chord music above if you need to, and just add in the syncopation.

> KCA_5_22

Rising and falling inversion strings

Swapping inversion groups to come down the keyboard is the next challenge. Here, the jump is more likely to happen between the I and IV chords.

> KCA_5_23 | KCM_5_23

Here's a descending version that covers the ground even faster.

| KCA_5_24 | KCM_5_24 |

Only the I–IV jumps are marked with the double-slash symbol.

More syncopated I–IV–V riff material

The aim is to get to the point where you can wander freely around the keyboard playing I (C), IV (F) or V (G) chords (according to the chord sequence) under whatever top (melody) note sounds right.

But as well as moving our triads across the keyboard, we want to break them up and pattern the hands in interesting ways. You started doing this in the Afro-jazz material in Module Four, and you will recognise some of the same techniques in the following examples.

These examples are not all fully written out – try to learn them from the preparatory exercises given and by copying the slowed-down MIDI files on MidiPiano. (The initial performance audios are up to speed at 150 bpm.)

Note that you can learn and play any of these right hand patterns over simple left hand minims or chords or with no left hand at all. In a band, for example, your bass player would be supplying the bass line.

Sample Riff 1

| KCA_5_25 | KCM_5_25 |

The build-up

The reference files for the build-up are all in one audio/MIDI file. Loop either of them, listen through a few times and see if you can keep up. There's a bar's rest between each line of music.

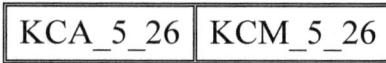

| KCA_5_26 | KCM_5_26 |

First, rehearse the underlying chords and practice the bass line

Then break the right hand triads up top two notes and the bottom note and 'waggle' them both ways up:

Now waggle the triads in quavers over simple bass line minims. Notice the difference in the second half of the line: the right hand thumb anticipates the new chord. This makes your playing sound more interesting.

Then the actual riff right hand over a simplified bass line:

The audio segues into the developed-bass-line version at practice speed.

Sample Riff 2

| KCA_5_27 | KCM_5_27 |

The build-up

This riff splits the C and F triads up outside notes, middle note, and the G triad one top note, two bottom notes. This little study drills the break-ups mechanically:

| KCA_5_28 | KCM_5_28 |

Sample Riff 3

This riff (right hand) is played an octave lower than written.

| KCA_5_29 | KCM_5_29 |

Build-up exercises

Always rehearse your 'underlying chords'. The fingering for the chords is right – if you want to play the actual riff as written. Drill the chords with easier fingering anyway.

| KCA_5_30 | KCM_5_30 |

Look at how the triads are broken up and devise a finger drill. It doesn't have to be 'music'.

| KCA_5_31 | KCM_5_31 |

Building up this level of finger dexterity is a long-term goal – 'little and often' will get you there.

In the meantime, play the simpler version:

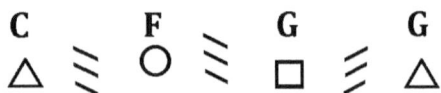

| KCA_5_32 | KCM_5_32 |

Sample Riff 4

It's easy to put new riffs together from rearranged parts an octave higher or lower.

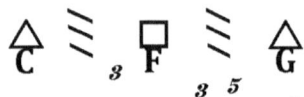

| KCA_5_33 | KCM_5_33 |

What you should really get from this riff however is the 'smoothing out' of the quaver-crotchet-quaver rhythm in the third bar.

First, get your underlying triads reliable.

| KCA_5_34 | KCM_5_34 |

Listen to these examples of the original syncopated then smoothed-out groups of three notes.

| KCA_5_35 | KCM_5_35 |

Even simpler:

| KCA_5_36 | KCM_5_36 |

To some extent, the smooth-out is just lazy fingers, but the three-over-two is also a characteristic feature of Latin rhythm. Play a straight minim in the left hand for now.

If you play a bass line under the tuplet, it will generally join in with the tuplet feel.

| KCA_5_37 | KCM_5_37 |

At some stage, you will want to cycle back through the other riffs and see if you can put some of the tuplet feel in them. The tuplet rhythm eventually becomes an option in all your playing, but it is especially valuable in this up-tempo Latin beat.

Broken chords, left hand triads and 'pedals'

Riff

| KCA_5_38 | KCM_5_38 |

Build-up

Find these three triads – anticipate the G chord.

KCA_5_39 | **KCM_5_39**

Break the chords up top, bottom, middle, top. The F chord only gets three notes because the G chord comes a quaver early. Rehearse without the bass line first, or just with simple minims.

T B M T T B M T   B   M T B M T   T B M T T B M T   B   M T

KCA_5_40 | **KCM_5_40**

You might want to experiment with other BMT orders, just to have options and give your playing variety. A mix (second half of the line) sounds good.

T M B T T M B T   B   M T B M T   T M B T T B M T   B   M T

KCA_5_41 | **KCM_5_41**

Work the bass line into the riff. Note that there's a BMT 'tweak' in the right hand in the second half – the top note of the last G chord is pulled fo4ward over the bar line to become last 'T' quaver in the third bar.

KCA_5_42 | KCM_5_42

Now find these left hand chords:

KCA_5_43 | KCM_5_43

Play them on beats 1 (2) & (3) (4), and tap out a rhythm on note G in the right hand.

KCA_5_44 | KCM_5_44

In classical piano technique, you always alternate two or three fingers for repeated notes. A good habit to get into – RH2 and 3 are recommended here.

A repeated or held note like this which disregards the changing chords in the chord sequence (the F chord, in this case – the G is not an F-chord tone) is called a 'pedal', after the foot pedals of the church organ. You can have 'pedals' in the bass (more usual) or in the treble, as here.

Here is the beat map for the syncopation above. Practice away from the keyboard, but try to use the right fingers and visualise the notes.

| KCA_5_45 | KCM_5_45 |

You don't have to follow the written music slavishly – just get something similar going that you can repeat over and over and start again reliably.

Try putting the broken chords over your new left hand chord style. Watch out for the right hand tweak in bar 2.

| KCA_5_46 | KCM_5_46 |

Of course, you can easily join up sections of the last two examples.

If you're playing in a group, you're likely to be playing 'comping' chords ('accompanying' chords) in the left hand. Eventually, you will want to be as good finding all the inversions of I, IV and V with your left hand (around middle C) as you are with your right.

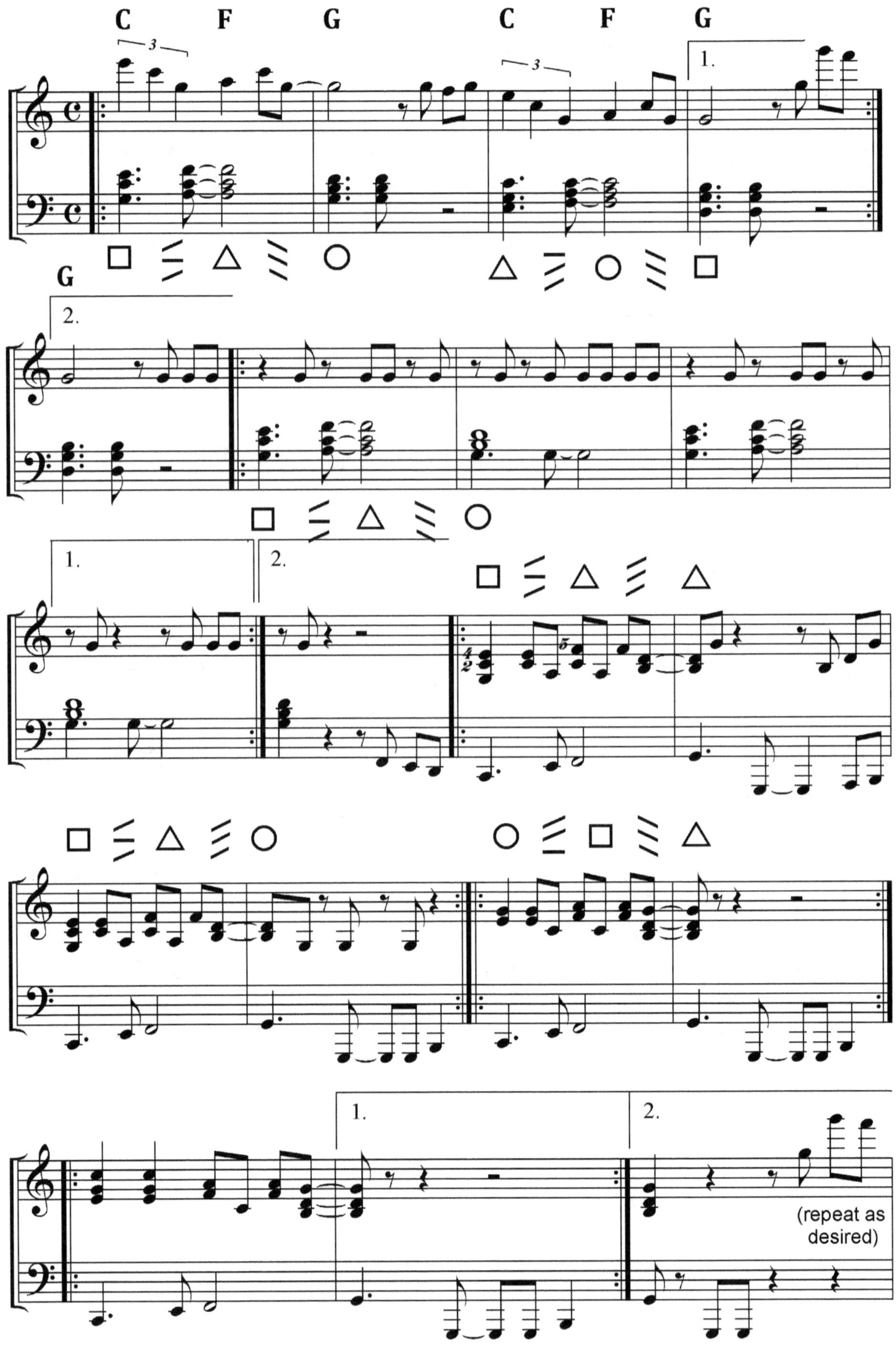

It

takes a while to learn to play these left hand chords off the beat. You see how much like conga-playing (drumming) modern keyboard style is – practice your tapping away from the keyboard whenever you can.

On the previous page, there's a final riff combining a selection of these latest elements. Notice the new triads in the left hand.

KCA_5_47	KCM_5_47

Summary

In this Key Chords module you have practiced moving between the inversions of the three most important chords in a key and put your skills to work with the pop classic, 'La Bamba'.

The more you play the riffs in this workbook, the more you will hear the I, IV, V chords in popular music and the easier you will find it to play along. If you have an electronic keyboard, you will be able to match your C position I–IV–V skills to any piece using the 'transpose' facility, and you can spend time fitting the chords to the rhythm of your favourite songs.

Module Six consolidates your knowledge to date by showing you how you can harmonise any melody note (scale tone) with I, IV and V chords. A start is also made transposing the I–IV–V changes into other keys.

Harmonising the Major Scale with I, IV and V

This module brings together what you now know about using the I, IV and V chords to harmonise all the notes of the major scale.

Scale tones I and IV combined

If we put the keyboards for our I (C) and IV (F) chords next to each other, we can see that five scale tones – 1, 3, 4, 5 and 6 – are supported by I and/or IV chords. (The C octave at the top isn't counted a second time.)

The circle, square and triangle inversion symbols show which inversions hang down from or prop up the 'supported' scale tones. The circle/square/triangle symbols are placed on the **top** note of the chord – the note you would hear as the melody. Add the next two shaded chord tones down (to the left) to get the three-note chord.

In the written music above, the scale degree melody notes are stems up; the supporting chords are stems down.

The line of chords from left to right makes a reasonable 'tune'. Practice.

Scale tones – I and V combined

If we do the same for our I (C) and V (G) chords, we find five scale tones are supported by I and/or V chords.

This also is a reasonably tuneful study.

Play through the I and IV and I and V lines of chords repeatedly. Work from the keyboards as much as from the music. Try to memorise the groups of chords. More important – understand 'why' those chords.

Note that this is not an academic exercise – you are rehearsing how top musicians and songwriters 'know' harmony.

Scale tones – I, IV and V combined

Adding all three keyboards together, we get the sum total of possible harmonies show in the next music example.

Work through, finding the line of chords.

Don't be put off by the written music. Start with middle C (scale degree 1) as the top note of a chord, and climb up eight white keys playing all the I, IV or V (C, F or G) chords that harmonise them – that you might find underneath them.

97

The scale degrees are numbered, so you can pick the chords used from the two previous keyboard diagrams. Only scale degrees 1 (= 8) and 5 have two possible supporting chords. Otherwise, it's a straight one chord per numbered scale degree.

| KCA_6_03 | KCM_6_03 |

You should ideally be able to find the chords from this information only:

| KCA_6_03 | KCM_6_03 |

This is where the circle, square, triangle symbols show their value. Remember the 'gaps' – the M's in the P-M-P counting. The original table is on page 45. Here is a vertical version.

Symbol*	⬡	P M P M P	△	**P** M M P M P	☐	P M **P** M M P
Type	Root position		First inversion		Second inversion	
In music	(music notation)		(music notation)		(music notation)	

* These symbols are used in Musicarta teaching material only. P = play, M = miss.

Harmonising the major scale, descending

Here's one possible way of harmonising (supporting with chords) the major scale, descending:

KCA_6_04 | KCM_6_04

Rehearse the string of chords, then see if you can reproduce them using just this information:

KCA_6_04 | KCM_6_04

Because scale degrees 1 (= 8) and 5 have two possible chords, we could also play:

KCA_6_05 | KCM_6_05

Rehearse thoroughly and then play from just this mark-up:

Practice the five music examples above thoroughly, using all the information sources:

- The keyboard diagrams and the shaded chord-tones, with the inversion symbols;
- In the written music: the chord symbols, Roman numeral chord symbols and the numbered scale degrees; and
- The numbered scale degrees plus the inversion symbols (circle, square, triangle) and the new P-M-P diagram.

The module riff – harmonising the major scale

The chords of the descending major scale are already 'nearly music'. Here's one possible practice chord sequence.

There is enough fingering in the music for you to play the right hand properly – outside fingers 1 and 5 where just the middle finger is given; fingers 2 and 1 under 4 or 3 as the given top finger.

To get started turning the chords into a riff, break up the notes of the chords into top, bottom, middle, top (T B M T) quavers. Example chords are written out, plus the non-standard bars. To avoid running out of fingers, you have to play 5, 4 over every chord change.

There are drum tracks at various speeds (in the 'Drums_KC_General' folder) to support your practising.

KC6_DT1/2/3_104/112/120

KCA_6_07 | KCM_6_07

Develop the riff a step further. (Read the notes below before attempting this.)

| KCA_6_08 | KCM_6_08 |

The lower stave shows the 'underlying chords' so you can see where the music is coming from. Don't try to play these chords with the left hand – it's not possible; play the bass line from the previous version instead. The more elaborate the music is, the more important it is that you stay connected with the simple underlying basics – or you will 'get lost' in the notes and just be copying.

Go through the numbered places in the music [(i), (ii) etc] to see how the riff has been 'jazzed up'. You will find:

   (i) Anticipated notes;

  (ii) Suspension-resolution used on the full-bar chords at the end of the line;

 (iii) Little 'joining up' figures (runs of notes); and

 (iv) Adding in the third where the chord is too bare.

This is just a study, with just enough development to make it sound acceptably modern. But it rehearses something that accomplished modern pop/rock keyboard players all share – knowing instinctively which chords in the key family can be used to harmonise which notes of the scale.

The accomplished modern pop/rock keyboard player can also play in keys other than easy all-white-key C. The next module tackles the task of playing all the I–IV–V material in two representative new keys – D and B♭ major, with two sharps and two flats respectively.

Summary

So far in the Musicarta Key Chords modules, you have:

- Learnt why we focus initially on the I, IV and V chords (Module One)
- Practised closest inversion pairs of the I and IV chords (Module Two)
- Practised closest inversion pairs of the I and V chords (Module Three)
- Put the pairs together in two I–IV–I–V–I chord progressions (Module Four)
- Learnt to jump between all three chords in a I–IV–V riff (Module Five)
- Learnt to harmonise all the major scale tones with I, IV and V (Module Six)
- Practised your keyboard syncopation skills in the module riffs, using advanced counting and together/left/right (TLR) analysis in beat maps.

Try to keep the overall Key Chords plan in mind so you know where you are – how far you've got and where you're heading – and can rightly celebrate your achievements so far.

Momentum counts in a learning process like this. If you take a long break from the work, consider a quick revision to bring your 'music brain' up to speed before continuing. Schedule in the Modules Two and Three 'optional extra' material, if you haven't covered it yet.

You will now go on to:

- Transpose the all-tones riff into two new keys (Module Seven)
- Incorporate the submediant vi chord into your key chord set (Module Eight)
- Transpose the new all-chord riffs into the two new keys (Module Nine).

Transposing I, IV and V

The ability to transpose – to change the key of some music (often just in your head) and play it higher or lower than the original – is one of the things that defines a really proficient musician.

Transposing is also an excellent way to learn musical material. When you try to transpose, you soon start to see the relative size of the steps between the notes or chord roots, plus many other pattern features. This makes music a lot easier to remember.

Pupils' ability to learn to transpose is generally underestimated, and the spin-off in terms of real keyboard skill and progress is significant.

The new keys

Playing the present all-white-key I–IV–V material in two new keys – D and B flat major – is a good start in transposing. Both keys have two black keys in the octave. D major is representative of the 'sharp keys' and B flat of the 'flat keys'.

Here are the D and B flat major key-specific keyboard diagrams which show what the keyboard looks like when you've taken the key signatures into account.

Playing scales is the traditional way of learning keys. The demonstration octave in the keyboard diagrams above has the scale fingering (right hand above, left hand below) for one octave – play the left hand an octave below the right and practice the octave to get the feel.

Using the Roman numeral system of naming chords to help in transposing

The Roman numeral system (RNS) names chords as if 'in any key', and is therefore extremely helpful in transposing. We already know that using just the notes of the major scale gives us a standard set of key chords:

At the moment, we're interested in just three chords:

I	IV	V
Tonic	Subdominant	Dominant

Here are the key-chord families in D and B flat major – the triads you can make from the major scale.

Key: D	D	Em	F#m	G	A	Bm	C# dim
RNS	I	ii	iii	IV	V	vi	vii°
Key: B♭	B♭	Cm	Dm	E♭	F	Gm	A dim

KCA_7_03	KCM_7_03

Copy the audio or MIDI files, and play the key-chord triads through in D and B flat. It feels very different with two accidentals (regular black keys) – you really have to get your fingers up on the keys to get to the chords.

I, IV and V in the new keys – key of D

The new three-chord I, IV, V families we need to learn are:

	Tonic I	Subdominant IV	Dominant V
Key: D	D	G	A
Key: B♭	B♭	E♭	F

Play the shaded notes right through the three keyboards from top left to bottom right.

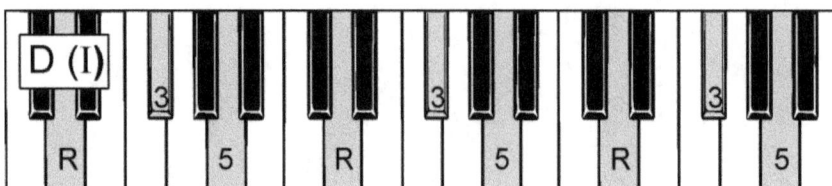

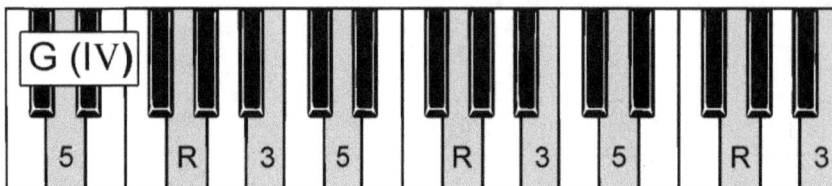

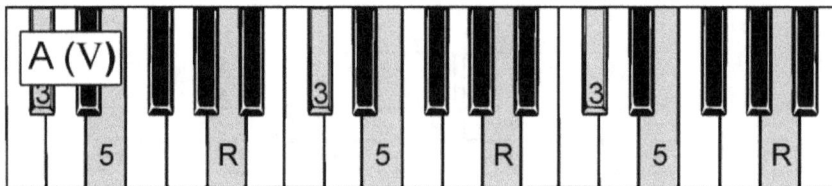

In the music, the notes affected by the key signature (the black keys) are circled.

The D chord tones

The G chord tones

The A chord tones

KCA_7_04	KCM_7_04

Key of B♭

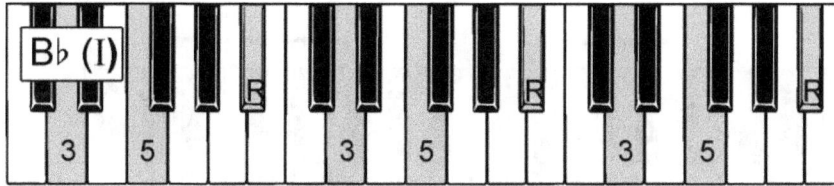

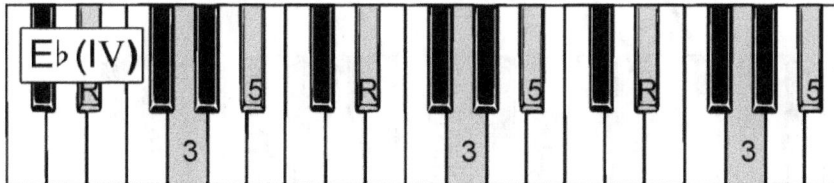

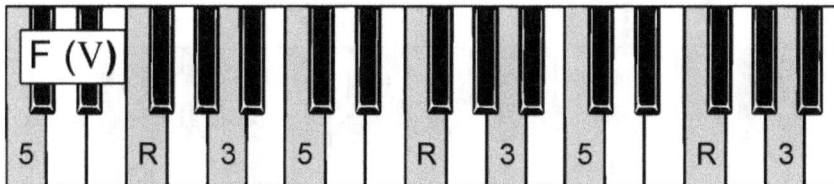

The B♭ chord tones

The E♭ chord tones

The F chord tones

The notes affected by the key signature, and therefore played on black keys, are circled.

| KCA_7_05 | KCM_7_05 |

Keep practicing until you physically recognise both the six sets of chord tones and the two sets of I-IV-V key chords.

Find I-IV-I-V-I in three places

Now find chords I–IV–I–V–-I in three places (nearest inversions). Note that the groups of closest inversions you're looking for (joined by the voice movement lines) can be anywhere (high or low) on the keyboard.

I-IV-I-V-I in D major

KCA_7_06 | KCM_7_06

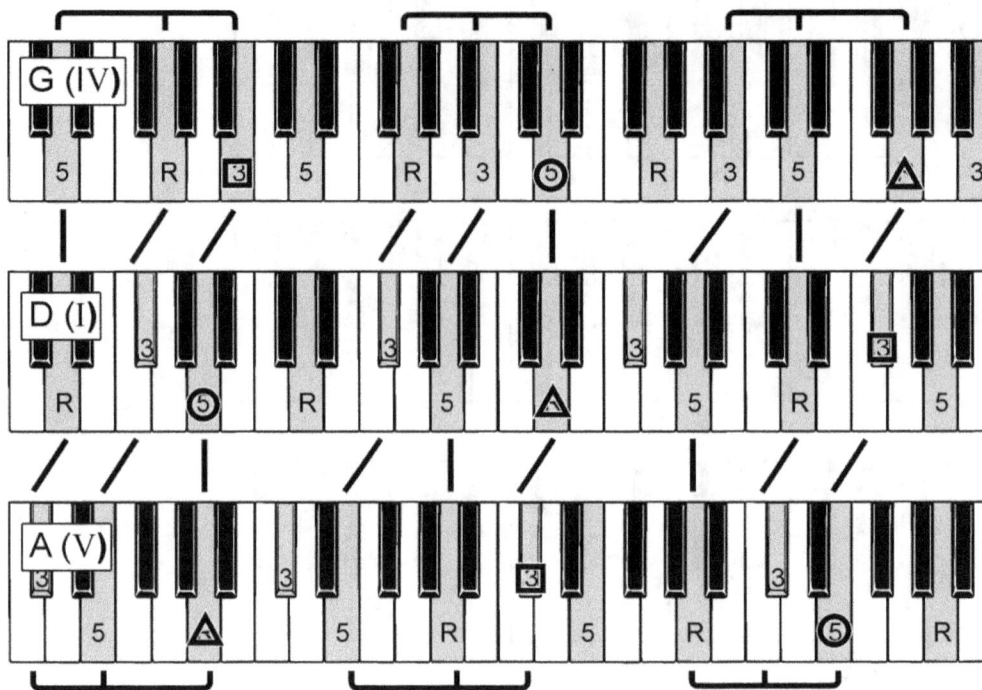

With the slash chord, you actually play chords D, G, D/A, A, D.

I-IV-I-V-I in B♭ major

KCA_7_07 | KCM_7_07

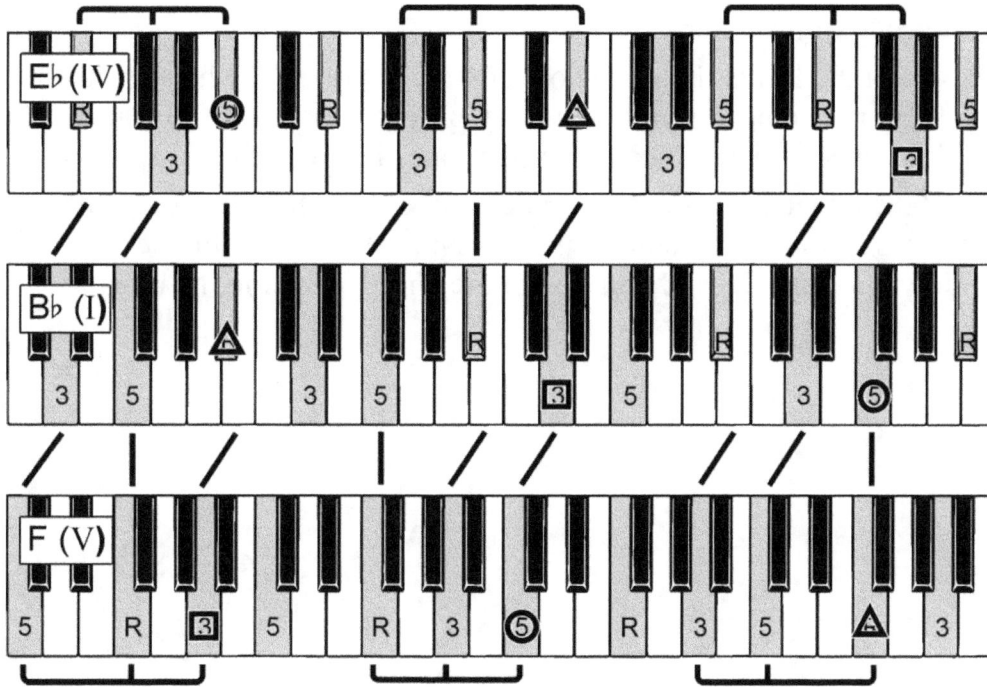

With the slash bass, you play B♭, E♭, B♭/F, F, B♭.

Find I-IV-V in three places

Now find I-IV-V, I-IV-V (the 'La Bamba' chords), where the second V chord takes you up to the next group of inversions.

You will start from the lowest I chord shown on the keyboards, whatever inversion it is. The keyboards are re-arranged so that you now play top-to-bottom. Because you swap sets of inversions, there are no voice movement lines between the IV and V chords.

You can 'read' the music just using the circle/square/triangle inversion symbols. The inversion symbols sit on the top note of the three-note triad. Add the next two shaded chord tones down (to the left) and you've got the chord shown in the music.

Creating your own drum tracks

There are several good free drum machines you can use to provide a metronome 'click track' for practising, or to make full drum backing tracks to support your playing.

In Drumbot (http://www.drumbot.com/projects/drumbot/), you assemble recorded samples in a very intuitive interface. You can save and re-load your tracks (projects) to work on them further and download them as .wav files to loop in Audacity – a really easy way to create drum tracks.

In Hammerhead (http://www.threechords.com/hammerhead/), a free, downloadable desktop application, and Drum Machine (http://www.onemotion.com/flash/drum-machine/), you build your beats by filling slots with sampled drum sounds. Hammerhead is a good entry-level asset. Drum Machine has attractive sounds, but you can't save or download your creations.

Key of D

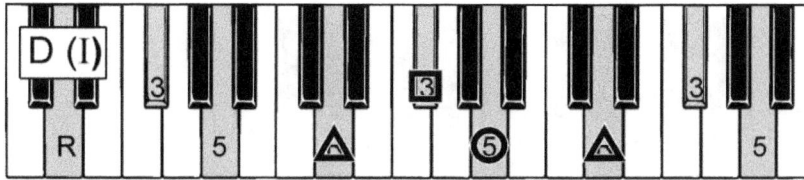

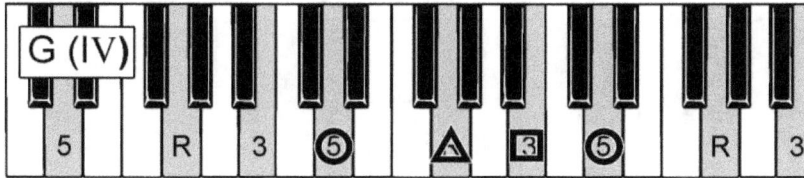

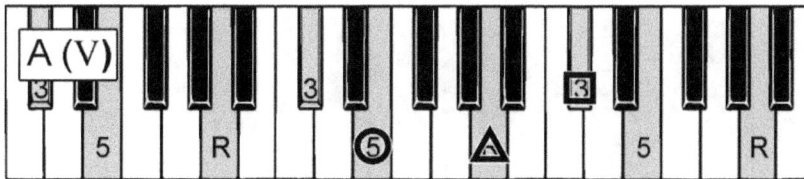

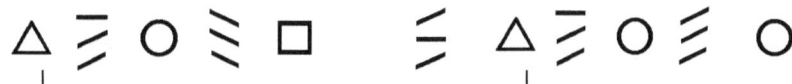

Key of B♭

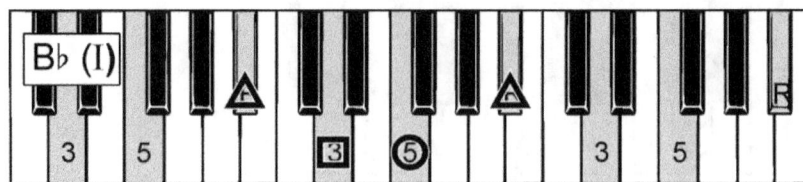

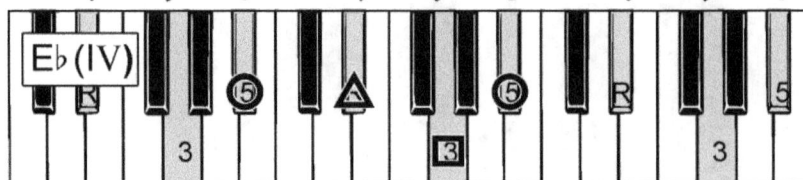

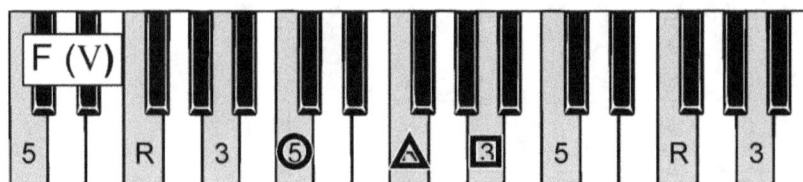

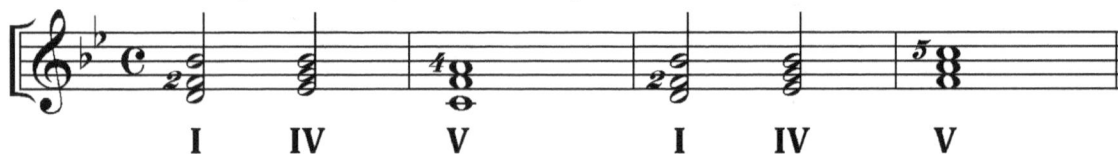

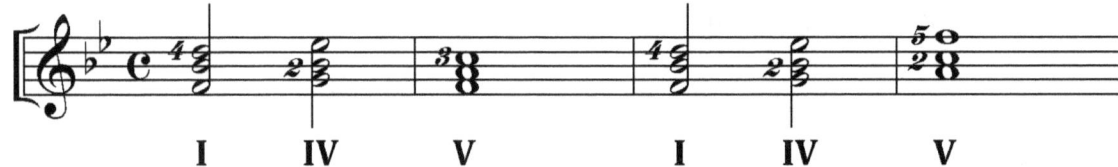

Now remind yourself of the Module Six 'Harmonising the Major Scale' riff.

| KCA_7_10 | KCM_7_10 | (re-use KC6 drum tracks) |

For transposing, the scale degree of the top note of the chord, the RNS name of the chord and the circle/square/triangle are what's important. So for transposing, you see:

Transposing into the new keys

Here are the three D major I, IV, V chord keyboards again. They are marked up with the D major scale degree numbers and the chord tone (R, 3, 5) numbers have been removed for clarity.

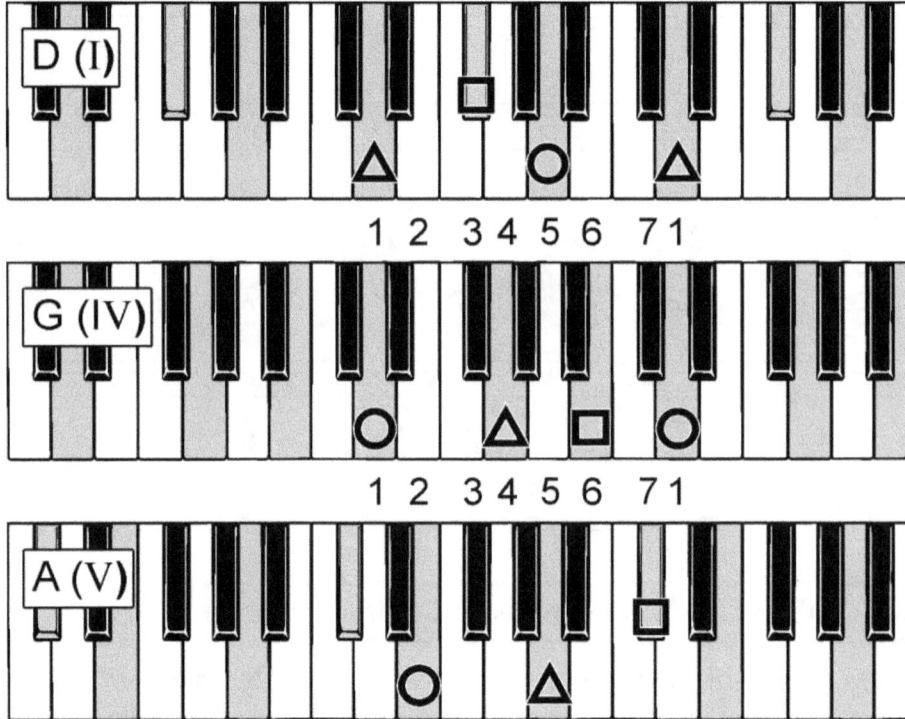

Note that the scale degree numbers are the same for all three chords/keyboards. They are the scale degrees of the key of D – the key you're playing in –counted from D to D.

The circle/square/triangle inversion symbols sit on the top note of their three-note triads. Add the next two (shaded) chord tones to the left to complete the chord.

Read the key-of-C I, IV, V chord sequence off the D major keyboards and you get:

| KCA_7_11 | KCM_7_11 |

(MS on next page)

Here are the three B♭ major I, IV, V chord keyboards, marked up with the B♭ major scale degrees and the inversion symbols.

Remind yourself: the string of right hand C major triads you are transposing is this:

Read the marked-up I, IV, V chords off the B♭ keyboards and you get:

| KCA_7_12 | KCM_7_12 |

Now you can develop the riff far as you like in the new keys.

Here's the first half of the Module Six riff development in our new key D major.

| KCA_7_13 | KCM_7_13 |

(The audio and MIDI files are for the whole riff.)

Here's the second half of the riff written out in B♭:

| KCA_7_14 | KCM_7_14 |

Practicing other material in the new keys

You can use MidiPiano to transpose the gospel material and the 'La Bamba' or any other MIDI files, so you can learn to play material you already know in other keys. (It's best to practice transposing music you already know.)

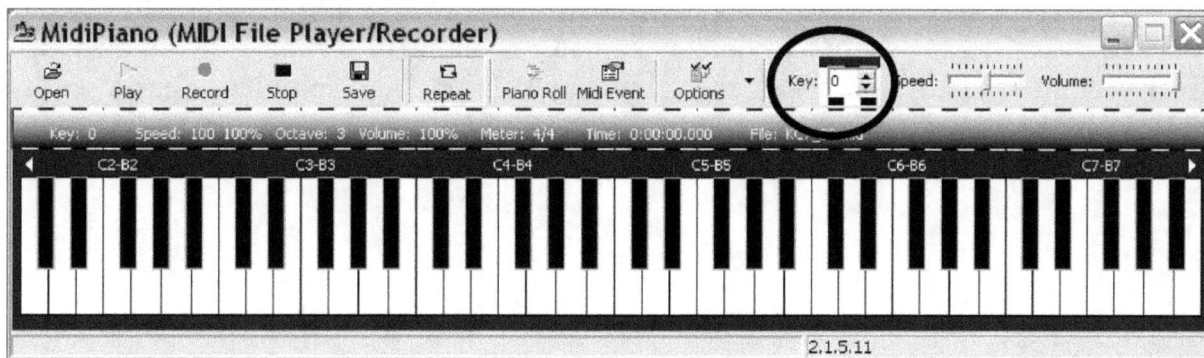

117

On MidiPiano, you see a control called Key (to the left of Speed). This control has up and down buttons. Each click on the buttons moves the output of the MIDI file up or down a semitone.

Try it out! Load any MIDI file, and whilst it's playing, click on the 'Key' up or down arrows. Instantly you'll hear the sound get higher or lower, and the keyboard starts playing the new notes.

So if you load, say, a La Bamba build-up in C and give the Key control two up-clicks – so that it reads 2 – you will see-and-hear the material in the key of D. Two down-clicks from original C will give you the material in B♭.

Here is a table showing how many clicks you need to play and hear Modules Two through Six MIDI files (which are in C) in other keys:

				▲	2	3	4	5	7	(up)
G	A♭	A	B♭	C	D	E♭	E	F	G	
(down)	-5	-4	-3	-2	▼					

Transposing is challenging at first, but, in time, practice makes any perplexing task routine. A lot of top-level musical skills are built through simple repetition, just like top-level sports skills.

As a keyboard musician, you are bound to find yourself, sooner or later, in a situation where some measure of transposing expertise is required, so put yourself on a regular transposing practice regime. Repeat Modules Two to Six of this workbook in D and B♭ by loading the MIDI files and clicking twice up or twice down on the MidiPiano 'Key' control arrows.

Learning by copying is a perfectly valid technique, but scale practice will more quickly teach you which piano keys belong in which musical keys – which black keys to play and which white keys to avoid, as shown in the key signatures. Get familiar with the contents of the 'Scales' tab at www.musicarta.com, and refresh your motivation regularly.

Summary

In this module, you have transposed the Module Six I, IV, V riff into D and B♭ major, two keys representing the sharp and flat key signatures. In the next module, you introduce the final Volume One key chord – vi, the submediant chord – and complete a basic set of chords which accounts for a large fraction of all the popular music every written.

vi (Six) – the Submediant (Relative Minor) Chord

In popular music chord progressions, after I, IV and V (One, Four and Five), the chord you are next most likely to hear is vi ('Six') – the submediant chord.

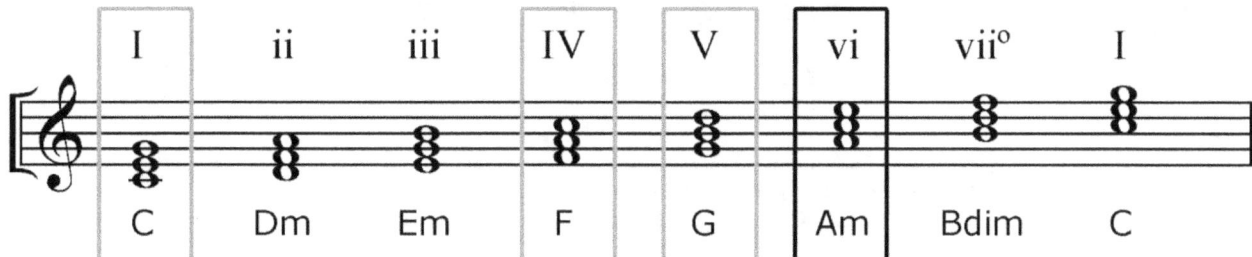

Chord Six is built on the sixth note of the major scale, which makes it a minor chord. This is why it is written 'lower case' (small letters) in Roman numerals – vi, not VI (upper case/capitals), which is for major chords.

Note that vi – the submediant – is sometimes called the 'relative minor (chord)'. This isn't strictly correct – the relative minor is a minor key with the same key signature as a given major key – but you will hear it and will have to translate it into 'vi – the submediant'.

Finding the new chord

In key C, the submediant (vi) chord is A minor, usually written 'Am' as a chord symbol.

You only have to change one note of a C major (I) triad to form and A minor (vi) triad – move any G up and you have an A minor chord.

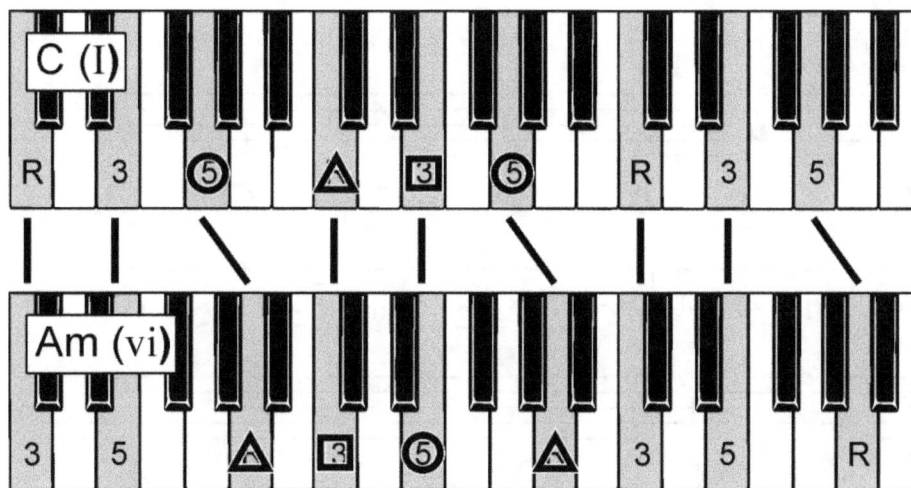

Use the circle/square/triangle symbols to help you play these pairs of nearest inversions.

KCA_8_01 | KCM_8_01

On the keyboards, the circle/square/triangle symbols sit on the top notes of the triads. In the music, the roots are arrowed.

Fitting the vi chord into the I, IV, V family

The most common position for the vi chord in our existing I, IV, V family is this mini chord sequence:

I–vi–IV–V

Use the I, vi, IV, V master keyboards [on the next page] to play the following 'lead sheet' music of the three sets of nearest inversions. (The first group repeats at the end.)

You have to pick your group of inversions according to the symbols, not just by reading the keyboards left to right.

KCA_8_02 | KCM_8_02

A 'lead sheet' (pronounced "leed sheet") give just the melody note – the top note of the right hand chord – with chord symbols. Musicarta material gives you the circle/square/triangle inversion symbols too. You fill out the written music by finding the inversion indicated for the C, Am, F or G chord on the keyboard diagrams.

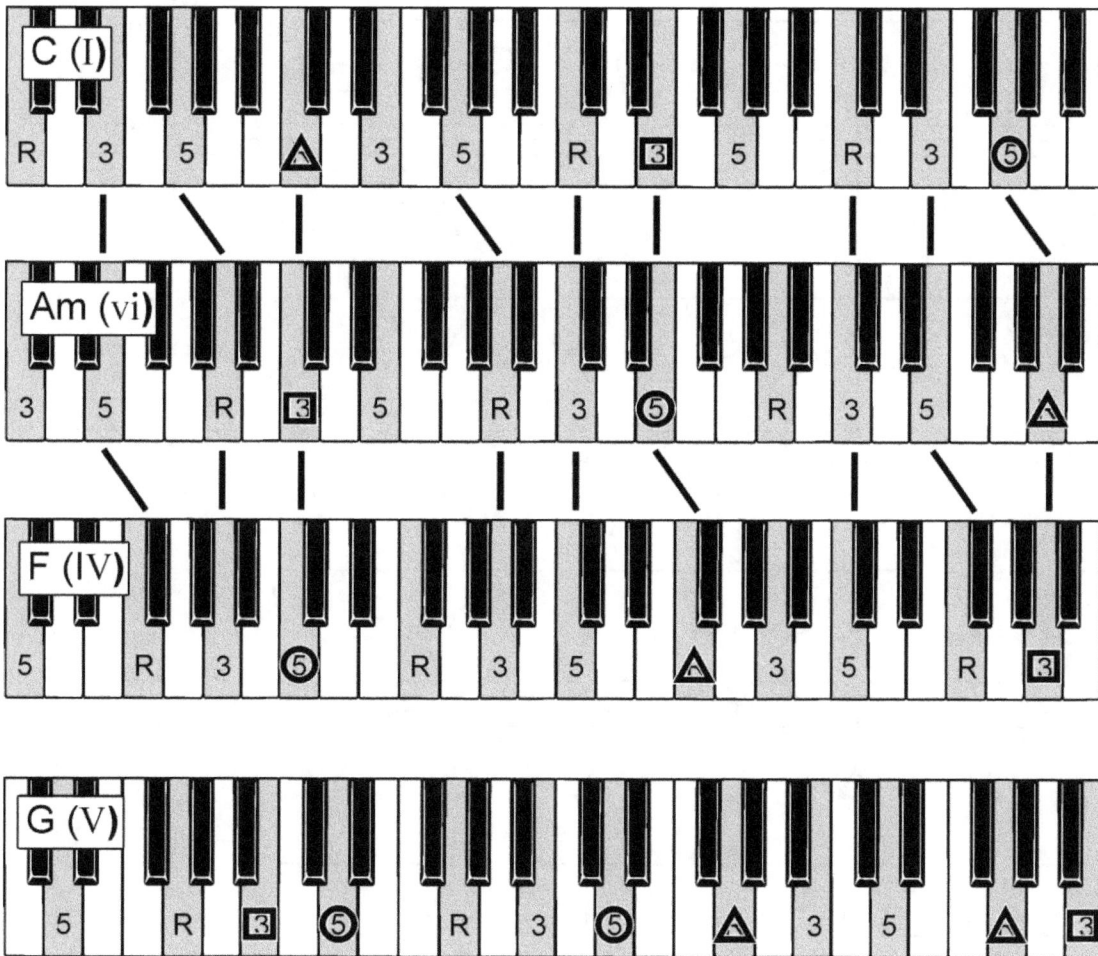

Next, use the 'next V chord up' to climb up through the sets of inversions.

KCA_8_03   KCM_8_03

Module Eight, Riff One

There are thousands upon thousands of ways of playing I, vi, IV and V. Once you can find these chords yourself, you will hear them everywhere in popular music. Here's one possible piano solo riff using the four chords.

KCA_8_04	KCM_8_04

The drums tracks for this riff are:

KC8_DT1 and 2_120

For a slower practice tempo use KC6_DT1 and 2 (104/112 bpm), or any slower-than-120 drum track.

Here's the Riff One chord sequence in a chart, with the inversion symbols.

○	△	□	△	○	△	□	△	
C	|Am	|F	|G	|C	|Am	|F	|G	|

△	□	○	△	△	□	○	△	
Am	||F	||C	|G	|Am	|F	|C	|G	|

□	○	△	○	□	○	△	○	
Am	|F	|C	|G	|Am	|F	|C	|G	|

Here's a rehearse-the-chords skeleton MS version.

| KCA_8_05 | KCM_8_05 |

The *8* below the single bass note means 'add a note an octave below', but you don't have to play and hold octaves (if you find it a stretch).

Now you have the notes, you add the rhythmic keyboard texture. Here's the written-out music for the first four bars of the riff:

The music is very complicated because the right hand splits into two, so in this module, you're going to learn the right hand texture using MidiPiano instead.

Look at this MidiPiano Piano Roll pane view of the first two bars.

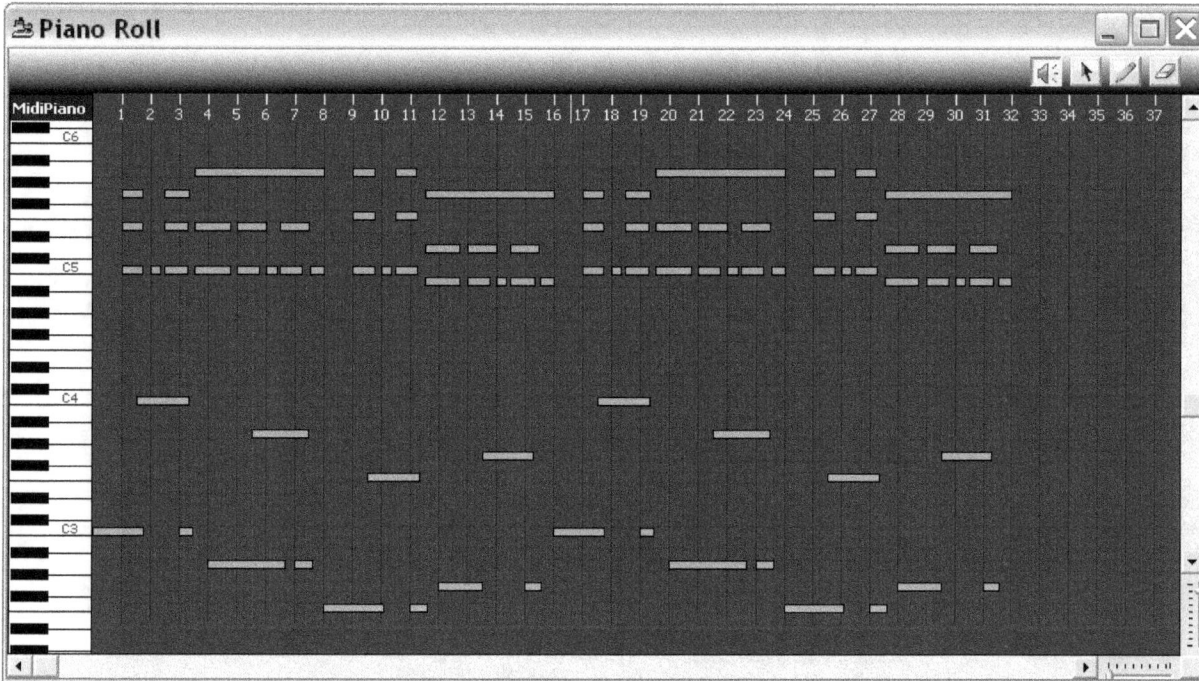

| KCA_8_06 | KCM_8_06 |

Dealing with the bass first (the green dashes); you can see the left hand simply bounces between the top and bottom notes of an octave root. If you can't stretch an octave (or it gets too tiring), just play a single bass note in the rhythm you hear.

Now take a closer look at the right hand (use the same audio/MIDI).

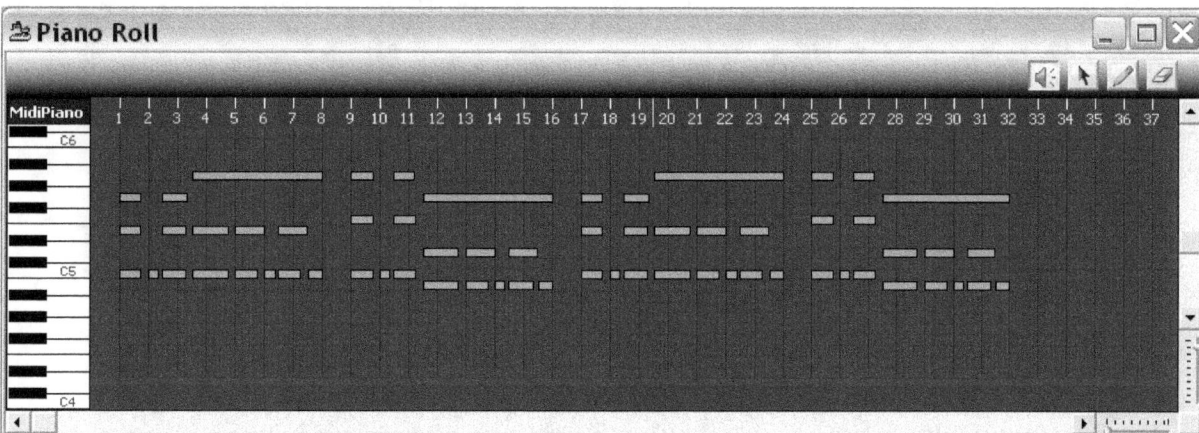

The chords you see there are:

O   △   □   △

C   Am   F   G

What you can tell is that the top note stays down the longest and the two underneath notes 'waggle'. This is, in fact, the 'maximum waggle' version. You could simplify the right hand a lot and still have an acceptable version. Look at/listen to this version:

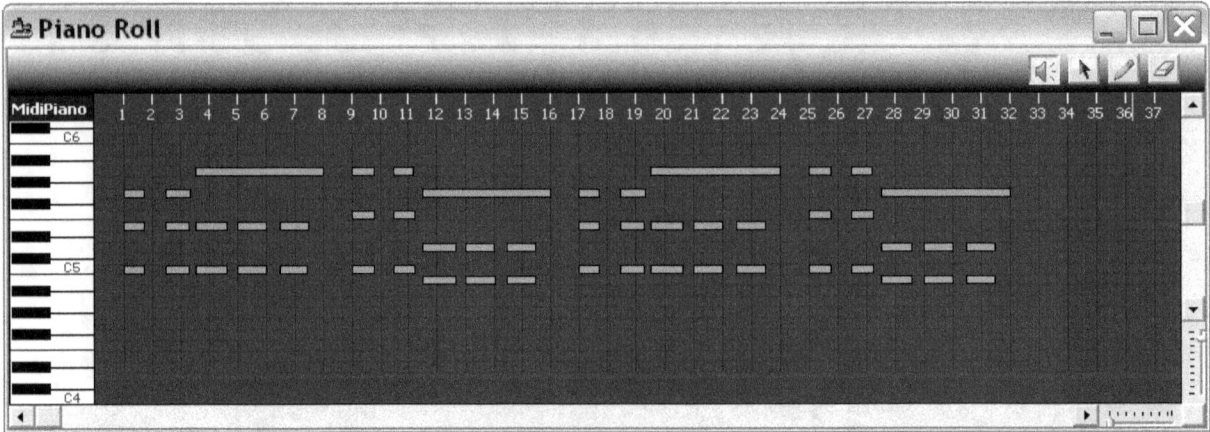

| KCA_8_07 | KCM_8_07 |

Here's a compromise version:

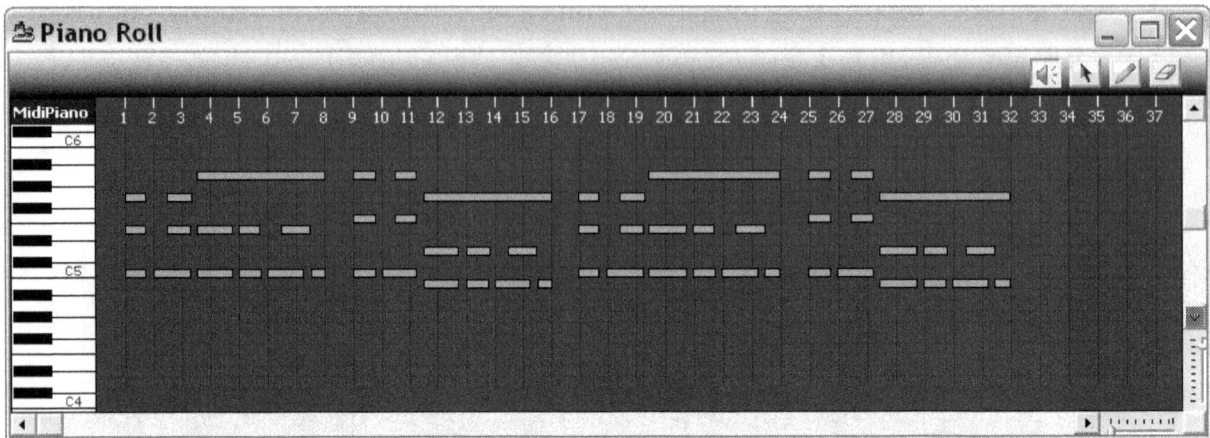

| KCA_8_08 | KCM_8_08 |

When you're learning something by ear like this (or even from the music), be ready to accept a not-quite-right-but-good-enough-for-the-time-being version. The version you can play all the way through is the one to value – the one you build on.

Notice that, when there's anticipation, it's the right hand thumb – the lowest note of the triad – that plays early – a useful 'hand-waggling' style to develop.

Here are some cleaned-up-and-simplified versions of the other two sections.

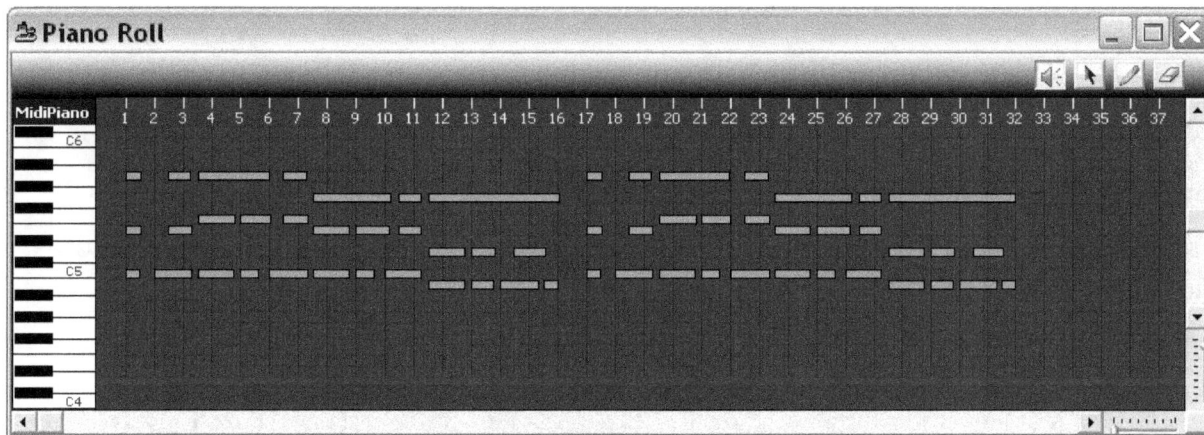

| KCA_8_09 | KCM_8_09 |

The chords you see (repeated) are:

△	□	○	△
Am	F	C	G

Not much different from the original. Find the inversion on your keyboard and imitate the texture ('waggle') by copying the pattern of broken lines.

The last section:

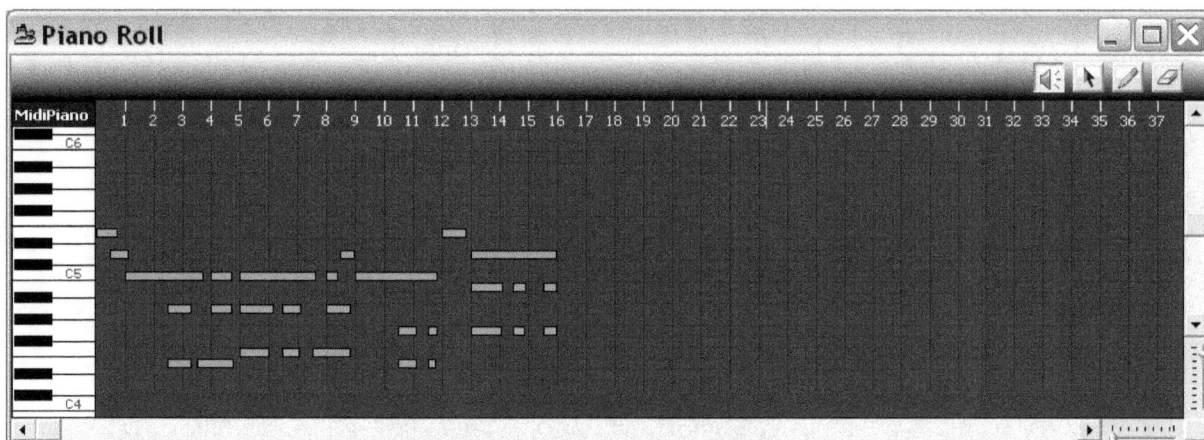

| KCA_8_10 | KCM_8_10 |

The chords are:

□	○	△	○
Am	F	C	G

Imitate the 'waggle'. Be ready to develop any different or easier 'just-for-now' version into a riff of your own!

More I, vi, IV, V material

The main module riff above covers two common arrangements of the I, vi, IV, V chords, as shown in the two boxes:

○	△	□	△	○	△	□	△
C	Am	F	G	C	Am	F	G
△	□	○	△	△	□	○	△
Am	F	C	G	Am	F	C	G
□	○	△	○	□	○	△	○
Am	F	C	G	Am	F	C	G

These are:

I	vi	IV	V	
C	Am	F	G		I–vi–IV–V

…and:

vi	**IV**	I	V	
Am	F	C	G		vi–IV–I–V

For practical purposes, that leaves one more arrangement to explore|

vi	IV	**V**	**I**	
Am	F	G	C		vi–IV–V–I

Here's a chord sequence using mainly that ordering, and the skeleton chords to practice.

△	□	△	□	△	□	△ O	△
Am	F	G	C	Am	F	G :C	G

△	□	△	□	□	□	△	△
Am	F	G	C	Am	F	G	F/G

O	O	△ O	□ △	△ O	□
F	G	C :F/C	G/C:F/C	C :F/C	G/C

Here are some skeleton chords for that chord sequence:

If you learn the chords and use MidiPiano intelligently, you should be able to play something like this performance.

| KCA_8_12 | KCM_8_12 |

Here's a nearly identical chord sequence, played in a triplet-feel country waltz style.

△ □ △ □ △ □ △ O △
Am │F │G │C │Am │F │G :C │G │

△ □ △ □ □ △ O O O
Am │F │G │C │Am │F │G :F │G │

△ O O △
F │G │F/C │C │

Here's a performance based on those chords:

| KCA_8_13 | KCM_8_13 |

Here are the skeleton chords for that performance:

KCA_8_12 | KCM_8_12

If you learn the chords and use MidiPiano to examine the performance closely, you should be able to play something like it. If you are motivated, you will definitely come away with a riff of some sort. All the reminders about the half-way-there riff or texture that you *can* play being worth more than an official finished version that you can't, apply here in strength.

(Remember to check MisterMusicarta YouTube regularly for relevant demo videos.)

Summary

In this module, you have added the final Volume One key chord to complete the I, IV, V, vi set. If you've mastered the theory and keyboard material, you're well on your way to understanding and playing a good part of the pop/rock repertoire. The next module formalises your I, IV, V and vi harmonising skills and tackles the necessary transposing tasks.

Harmonising the Major Scale with I, IV, V and vi

Here is a collection of I, IV, V and vi keyboards which shows all the triads of those chords occurring over an octave of C major scale tones. The circle/square/triangle symbols sit on the top note of the triad they represent. You add the next two shaded chord tones to the left to make up the triad.

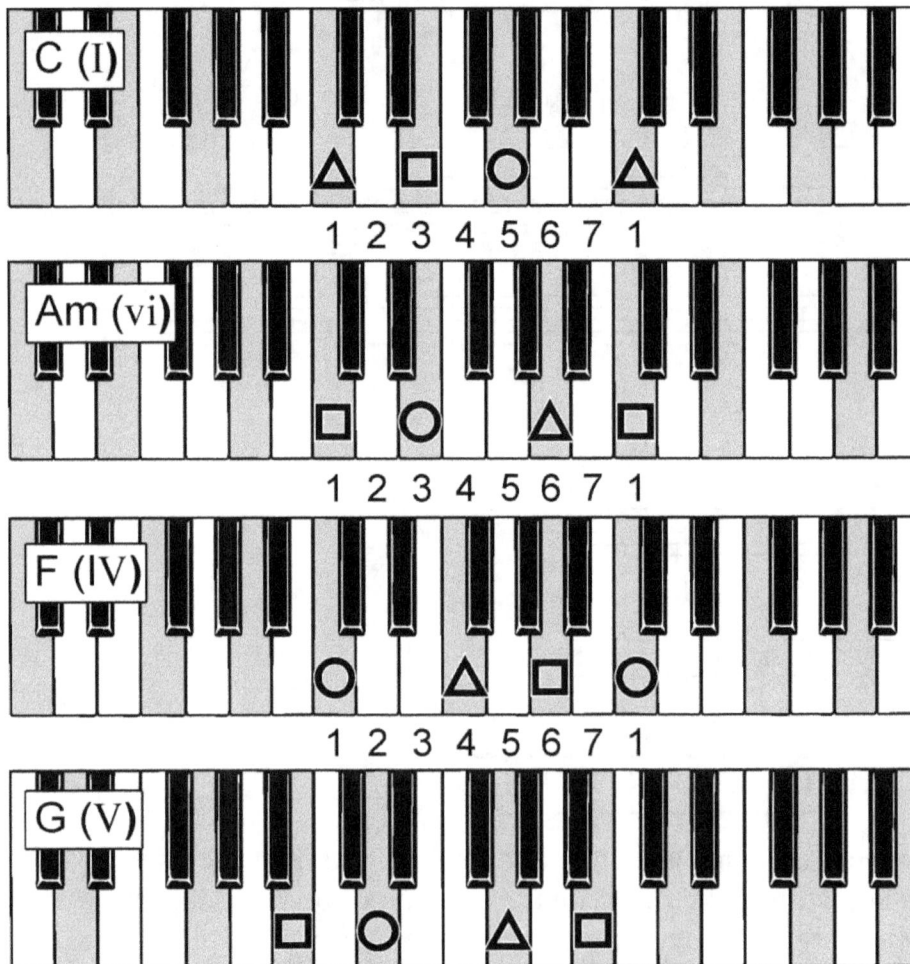

On the next page, you will find the music for a string of triads which uses all these potential harmonies. If you don't read music particularly well, find the chords using the numbered C major scale degrees, the chord symbols and the circle/square/triangle symbols. (Good sight-readers should take this information in too.)

Learn this string of triads.

Note that you do not start on the tonic (chord I) – the chords are arranged to make a riff.

| KCA_9_01 | KCM_9_01 |

Here is a simple development of these basic triads created by breaking up the chord into bottom, middle and top notes, and with a bit of anticipation. You don't use the final I chord (except perhaps to finish), and you repeat the last three chords

| KCA_9_02 | KCM_9_02 |

The skeleton chord mark-up of that music is on the next page. Break the chords up according to the B-M-T (bottom-middle-top) mark-up.

Now you have a riff harmonising a descending major scale using all the possible I, IV, V and vi chords.

The full written-out right hand music is on the next page, but you will gain far more in terms of creativity if you work your performance out from this BMT mark-up.

For an easier version, play just the top note of the chord where the full chord is given.

I, IV, V and vi in D

Adding the submediant (vi) chord to our existing I, IV, V chords gives us these new chord families:

	Tonic I	Subdominant IV	Dominant V	Submediant vi
Key: C	C	F	G	Am
Key: D	D	G	A	Bm
Key: Bb	Bb	Eb	F	Gm

In keys D and Bb, the new chords are B minor (Bm) and G minor (Gm).

Key: D	D	Em	F#m	G	A	Bm	C# dim
RNS	I	ii	iii	IV	V	vi	vii°
Key: Bb	Bb	Cm	Dm	Eb	F	Gm	A dim

Transposing the module riff into D and Bb will improve your understanding of 'harmonising' and your ability to hear the chords being used in popular music.

To make finding the new submediant chord in D easier, first revise the key of D major by playing the D major scale. The aim is to build a mental picture of a 'keyboard in D' with only the D major scale tones showing.

D major

D E F# G A B C# D   © R. A. Chappell 2012

1 2 3 1 2 3 4 5
5 4 3 2 1 3 2 1

www.musicarta.com

F# C#

| KCA_9_03 | KCM_9_03 |

Then, using the I, vi, IV, V in D keyboards on the next page, find (to start with) the inversions of the new vi chord (B minor) closest to the three inversions of D major.

Notice that you only have to move any note A in a D chord up one scale tone and you have a B minor chord. Next, find the three closest-inversion I–vi–IV–V chord groups

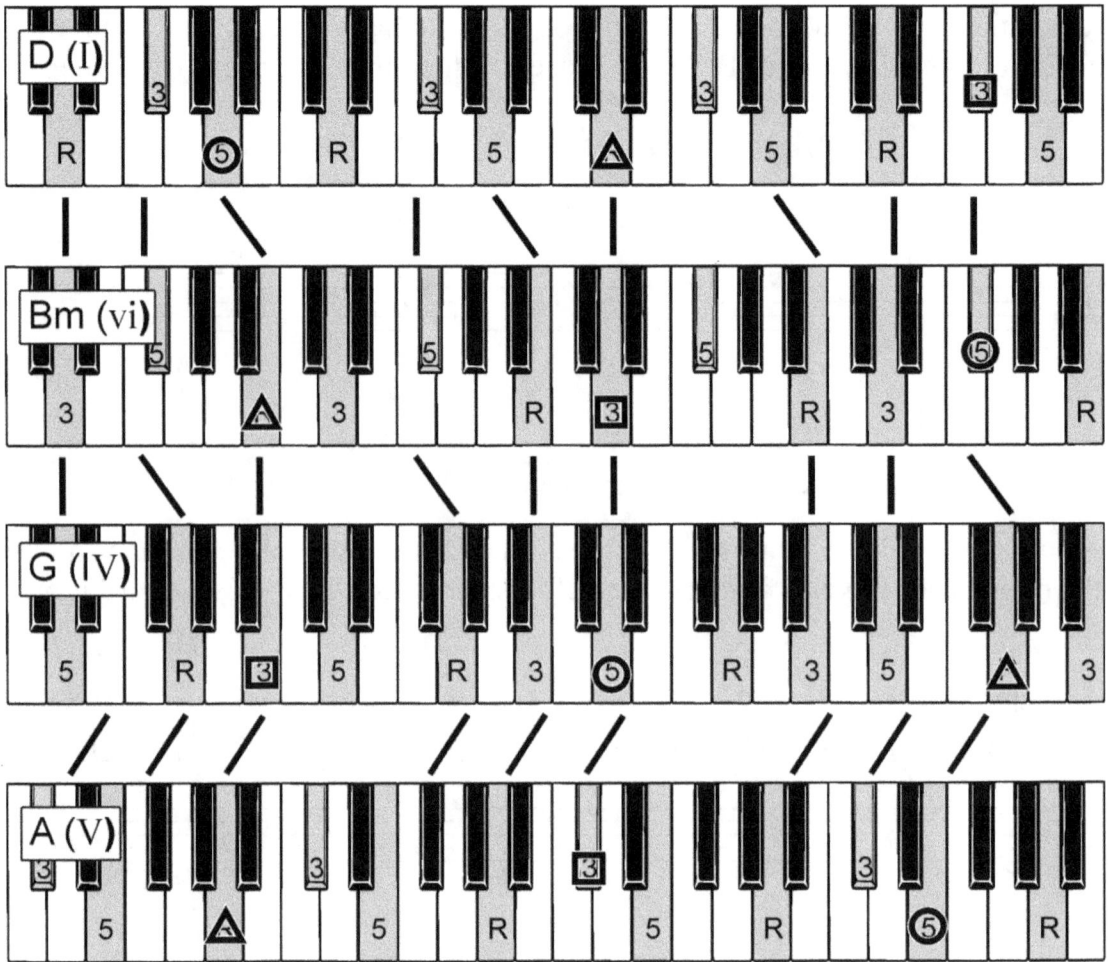

| KCA_9_05 | KCM_9_05 |

Remember, the groups of chords shown could be anywhere on the keyboard.

Next, use the keyboard illustration below to harmonise a descending octave of the D major scale.

(Remember, the circle/square/triangle symbols sit on the top note of the triad they represent. You add the two shaded chord tones to the left to make up the chord.)

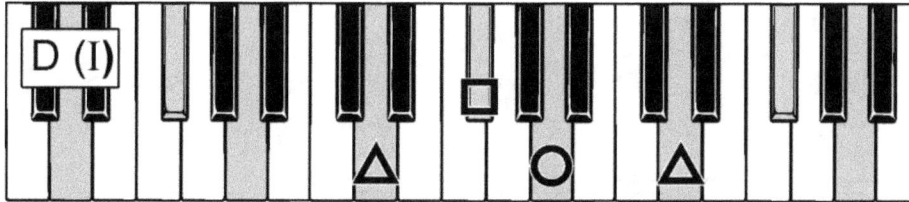

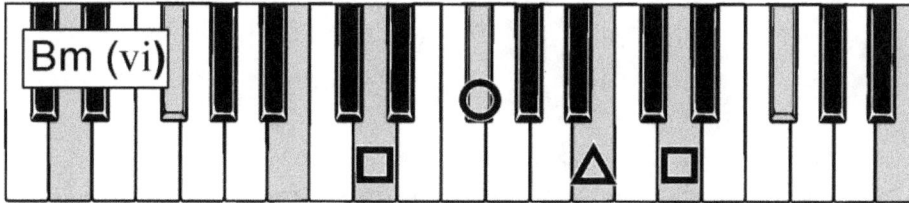

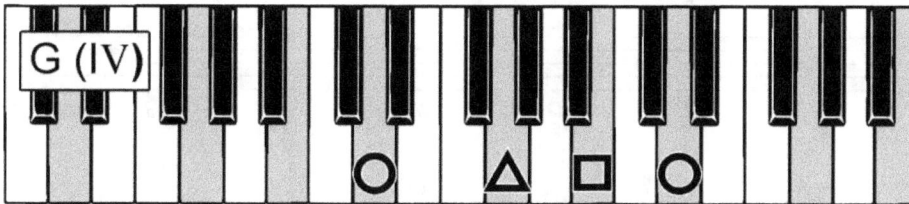

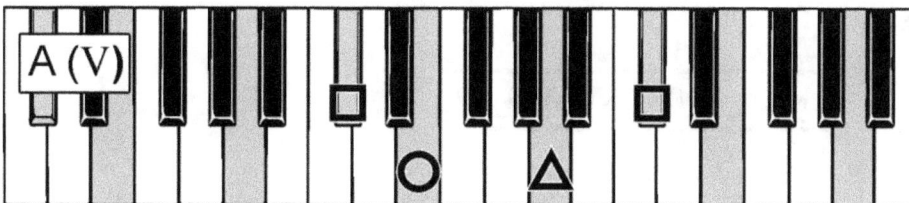

| KCA_9_06 | KCM_9_06 | KC9_DT1 (or 2)_104 |

Now play the harmonising riff in D:

| KCA_9_07 | KCM_9_07 |

A second I, IV, V, vi riff

Here's another possible triad string which harmonises all the C major scale tones using I, IV, V and vi. It's an octave higher than the previous riff. Supply left hand roots – also an octave higher.

KCA_9_08 | KCM_9_08

Playing the riff in B♭

You're going to play a riff using I–IV–V–vi chords in B♭ next, so refresh your memory of the B♭ scale and its 'key-specific keyboard'.

KCA_9_09 | KCM_9_09

Now use the keyboard illustration and the skeleton-chord music manuscript on the following pages to transpose the riff chords into B♭. You will probably find the MidiPiano performance the most help in working it out.

KCA_9_10 | KCM_9_10

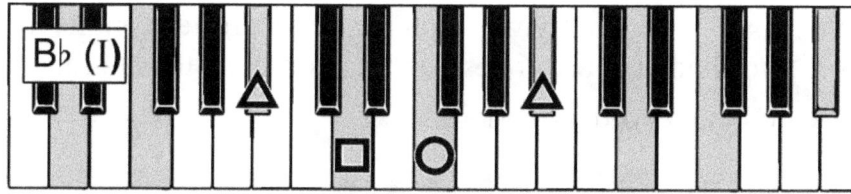

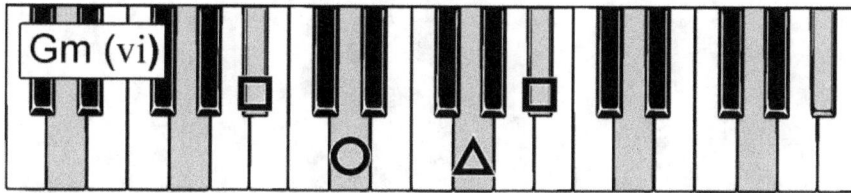

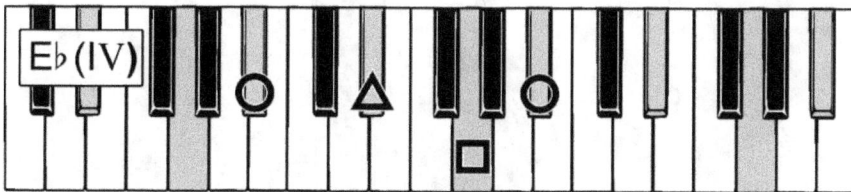

Remember, the circle/triangle/square inversion symbols on the keyboards are on the top note of the triads: add the next two shaded chord-tones down to complete the chord.

Here what the riff (in B♭) based on that chord string looks like.

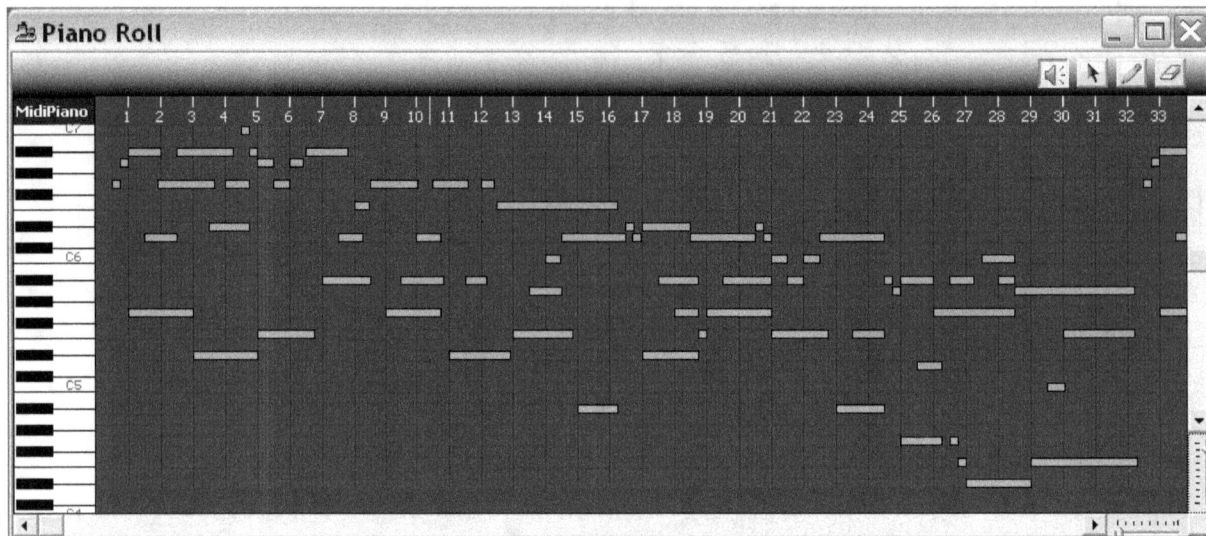

| KCA_9_11 | KCM_9_11 |

You hear immediately that the melody is much more developed than the first riff in the module.

The MS showing the melody and – stems down – the few chord tones you need to 'fill out' the right hand part is on the next page. The MS of the actual performance is on the page after that (page 148)

You might find that MidiPiano's Piano Roll pane actually provides a more-easily grasped picture of the actual performance: The illustration shows just the first eight bars. If you watch-and-listen enough times, you will see how the stems-down chord tones in the MS are used to fill up the quaver slots in the right hand where there's no melody note. This is the essential solo pop-styles technique.

Note that the counting is only for the right hand/melody.

The full written-out right hand part is on the next page. (Note that relying on the written music will not turn you into a creative musician!). In this version, the counting shows only where something <u>doesn't</u> happen in the right hand (main counts only).

A second B♭ arrangement

Here's another arrangement of the same tune.

| KCA_9_12 | KCM_9_12 | KC9_DT3_98 |

The chords are in the left hand. They aren't all plain triads. Here they are, written out:

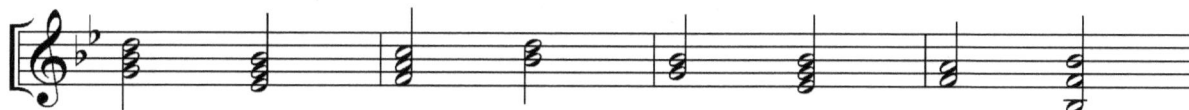

You will remember that all-line-note or all-space-note triads are root position triads, so the bottom note is the root. There are simple thirds (two-note chords) in the left hand too. In this study, the bottom note of the third is always the root/name-note, but you can't assume that will always be the case.

There are two other chord shapes here:

- A four-note chord, where the root is repeated above a root-position triad, so it's both the bottom and the top note; and
- A three-note chord consisting of the root, fifth (top note of a root position triad) and the root repeated 'at the octave'.

Here's the bottom line of the left hand chord music again, with all the roots arrowed:

If there isn't a slash-chord chord symbol, the bottom note of any left hand chord is probably the root (name-note), and you can build your left hand chords using some or all of the chord tones above it with reasonable confidence.

Here's the full MS for the new riff:

Read the music alongside the MidiPiano performance for clarity:

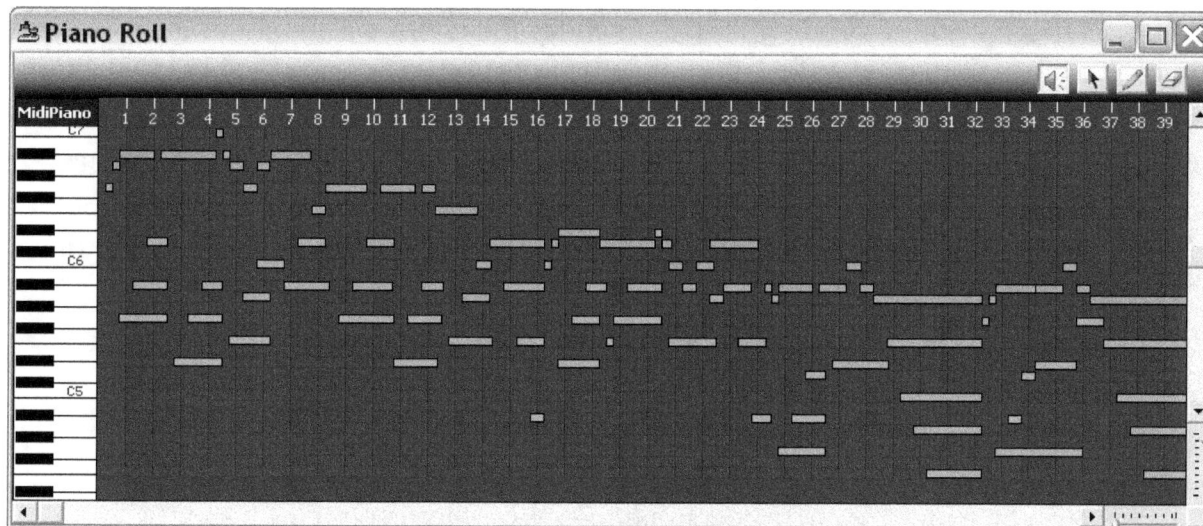

| KCA_9_12 | KCM_9_12 |

In closing

In this Key Chords module you have seen how any scale tone can be harmonised with an inversion of I, IV, V or vi, and have played a number of I, IV, V and vi keyboard riffs.

If you have worked through the last two modules thoroughly, you will have played the four chords in D and B♭ as well as simple all-white-key C. This is a major accomplishment by any standards. If you have understood where the chords come from and how to find them in a key, you have grasped a significant fraction of the harmony of popular music.

In the course of working through this first Key Chords volume your 'musical ear' will have improved considerably, too. You should expect to 'hear' the four chords in popular music – that is, to realise you're listening to I, IV, V and vi chords, even if you don't know which actual chords they are. (This is the value of persevering with the Roman numeral system and music theory methods of naming chords.)

You will find your ability to work out what chords are being used in a song has improved, too – I, IV, V and vi really are the songwriter/pop composer's first choice, most of the time.

Going forward from here

For the most thorough grounding, you would re-run Module Two to Six in D and B♭ major, and, if you didn't do so at the time, work through the Module One and Two optional extra material.

Once you are thoroughly at home with the first four key chords, the other chords will fall into place by themselves. There are only two – ii and iii (D minor and E minor in the key of C). If you want to go ahead and build your chord vocabulary yourself, identify the chord tones (using the Keyboard Chord Generator PDF if necessary) and work out which scale degrees the new chord can harmonise. Then try the chord out in any of the 'harmonising the major scale' riffs. Chord iii substitutes well for V (they share two chord tones), and ii for IV (for the same reason).

In harmonic terms – and in terms of your own study going forward – next steps include:

- Playing in minor keys (i, iv and V). You can use the Keyboard Chord Generator PDF to turn I and IV into minor chords i and iv – V stays unaltered. (Note that the module riffs won't sound as good. See the note regarding Modes, below.)

- Completing the key chords set by finding and incorporating ii and iii (as discussed above).

- Exploring the circle of fifths – starting with I–vi–ii–V.

- Understanding seventh chords. Seventh chords add impetus to circle of fifths cadences. You can learn about seventh chords via Chords on the Musicarta navbar.

- Making the minor key chords major. This is the first departure from diatonic, unaltered key chords. Major II, III and VI chords add impetus to circle of fifths cadences. Example: I–III–vi … or I–VI–II–V.

- The modes offer a great parallel source of harmony and chord sequences – especially for minor keys. Use the Modes tab on the Musicarta site navbar.

Looking forward, Musicarta offers a number of other possible study threads. The Pyramids Variations and the Canon Project are available as digital home study downloads – see the relevant tabs on the site navbar. The Modes series and an introduction to piano boogie and blues called the Moving Pair are still, at the time of printing, 'free to air'. There are numerous other freestanding 'practical theory' pages to help you discover the harmonic mechanisms of popular music and the levers to pull to get them going.

No creative musician's development takes a dead straight line. There is always some doubling-back, some criss-crossing and re-crossing of old territory, periods of pure slog and "Aha!" moments when the penny drops. The only constant is persistence; coming back time after time, 'joining the dots' and paying one's dues. For those who are called to it, the rewards – intellectual, emotional, spiritual even, that warm feeling when you realise that you can, finally, do it – are well worth it.

Organise your effort and embark, and you can rest assured that the journey on its own will enrich you beyond expectation!

Musicarta KEY CHORDS Volume I

- *Which chords should I learn?*
- *Which chords go together?*
- *How should I learn them?*

The chords in a song or piece of popular music aren't random. Chords group naturally in 'keys' and are made up from the notes of the scale of that key. The essential key chords number just six – three major and three minor. Of the two groups, the major chords are reckoned to sound 'happier', and are preferred.

Guitarists routinely learn this group of three major chords – C, F and G or E, A and B (I, IV and V – tonic, subdominant and dominant) – as a unit, and are quickly playing songs with them. Musicarta Key Chords aims to make this just as easy (and as much fun!) for the keyboard player.

Even simple chords, though, can appear in three 'inversions', each with a different note at the top. At a minimum, then, the proficient modern keyboard player needs to be able to find and move between a total of nine triads.

Musicarta Key Chords breaks this task up into easy bite-sized pieces, practising pairs of chords first in credible modern keyboard riffs. The pairs of chord are then combined in I–IV–V chord sequences, and finally the 'most likely' minor chord is added and the resulting possibilities explored.

The four chords covered in Volume One (I, IV, V and vi) account for a sizeable fraction of all popular music written, so you are bound to start hearing what chords are being used in lots of mainstream popular music.

Numerous illustrations and other conventions make reading music optional. Audio (MP3) of all the musical examples are available in a free supporting download package, along with the MIDI files and a free MidiPiano virtual keyboard app (Windows only) which enables you to see-and-hear what to play at your own speed.

Drum tracks to support your practicing and inspire your improvisations are also included in the free download.

Great for ambitious young keyboard players, classical cross-over students and adult piano re-starters/continuers. An ideal supplement to traditional piano lessons, and perfect continuing education for semi-pro and pro musicians.

Musicarta – a methodical approach to creative keyboard skills and repertoire. Visit www.musicarta.com and MisterMusicarta YouTube.

www.ingramcontent.com/pod-product-compliance
Lightning Source LLC
LaVergne TN
LVHW081316060426
835509LV00015B/1543